PYTHON

DATA SCIENCE

An Ultimate Guide for Beginners to Learn
Fundamentals of Data Science Using Python

CHRISTOPHER WILKINSON

Table of Contents

Introduction

Python is a well-known, high-level object-oriented programming language that is used by many software designers and data scientists across the globe. Guido van Rossum structured this in 1991, and Python Software Company has further developed it. Despite the fact that there were many OOP languages, the principal reason to build this language was to underscore code coherence, and logical and numerical processing (for example NumPy, SymPy, Orange). Python's syntax is simple and short. It is an open-source and versatile language that supports a large standard library.

Python is a broadly useful programming language that is well known for information science. Organizations worldwide are using Python to collect bits of knowledge from their information and addition a focused edge. In contrast to other Python instructional exercises, this comprehensive book on Python is explicitly for data science. It has a collection of amazing approaches to store and control information and accommodating information science apparatuses to direct your own examinations.

In the contemporary world, every business is focused on data security, management, and utility. All the renowned companies are playing with data through complex Python algorithms to store, manipulate, and process data to get useful information and to use it materially to benefit the business. Have you ever thought about Facebook pixels to re-target you on your profile page with the same product you viewed on an e-commerce website? Or Google's recommendations based on a place you visited previously? Nowadays, Android Speech Recognition and Apple Siri understand your speech signals with accuracy and respond to you accordingly. In all these high-tech products, there are algorithms and complex codes of machine language structured by Python.

This book "Python Data Science," an Ultimate Guide for Beginners to Learn Fundamentals of Data Science Using Python, I offer an extraordinary approach toward learning this high-level language to equip you with a complete method of using Python for big data management. As technology is growing fast, every organization requires a highly efficient system for processing data to achieve desired results. It is a detailed book with a comprehensive knowledge of data science, Python data structures, standard libraries, data science frameworks, and predictive models in Python. .

Chapter 1

Basics of Python for Data Science

1.1 What is Data Science?

Data science is a gathering of different instruments, data interfaces, and calculations with AI standards (algorithms) to find concealed patterns from raw data. This data is put away in big business data distribution warehouses and utilized in inventive approaches to create business value.

A data examiner (analyst) and a data scientist are unique. An analyst attempts to process the data history and clarify what is happening. Whereas a data researcher needs different propelled calculations of AI (algorithms of machine learning) for an event of a specific occasion by utilizing analysis.

1.2 Python and its History

Python is a translated, high level, universally useful programming language. Developed by Guido van Rossum and first discharged in 1991, Python's plan reasoning accentuates code clarity with its eminent utilization of critical whitespace. Its language develops and object-arranged methodology plan to enable software engineers to compose clear, sensible code for small and big scale projects.

Python was first developed in the late 1980s as a successor to the ABC language. Python 2.0, discharged in 2000, presented highlights, like rundown perceptions and a trash gathering framework, fit for gathering reference cycles. Python 3.0, discharged in 2008, was a noteworthy modification of the language, and much of the Python 2 code doesn't run unmodified on Python 3. Language designer Guido van Rossum carried sole duty regarding the undertaking until July 2018, yet now shares his administration as an individual from a five-man directing council.

1.3 Unique Features and Philosophy

Python is a versatile programming language that supports Object-Oriented Programming (OOP) and other practical computer program languages. Initially it was not designed for data science, but as field, professionals started using it for data analysis and it became a priority for data science. Many different standards are bolstered utilizing expansions, including a plan by contract and rationale programming. Likewise, it includes dynamic name goals (late authoritative), which tie technique and variable names during system operations. It has channel, guide, and decrease capacities, list understandings, word references, sets, and generator expressions. The standard library has two modules that actualize useful devices acquired from Haskell and Standard ML.

As opposed to having the majority of its usefulness incorporated with its center, Python was intended to be profoundly extensible. This reduced measured quality has made it especially well known as a method for adding programmable interfaces to existing applications. Van Rossum's vision of a central language with a huge standard library and effectively extensible translator originated from his dissatisfactions with ABC, which upheld the inverse approach.

Python makes progress toward a less complex, less jumbled language structure and punctuation, while allowing engineers to make decisions in their coding approach. As opposed to Perl's "there is more than one approach to do it" proverb, Python grasps a "there ought to be one—and ideally just one—clear approach to do it" plan. Alex Martelli, from the Python Software Foundation and Python book writer, states that "To depict something as 'sharp' isn't viewed as a compliment in the Python culture".

Python's engineers attempted to maintain a strategic distance from untimely advancement, and reject patches to non-basic pieces of the CPython that would offer minimal increments in speed at the expense of clarity. When speed is significant, a Python software engineer can move time-basic capacities to expansion modules written in dialects. For example, C, or use PyPy, an in the nick of time compiler. Cython is likewise accessible, which makes an interpretation of a Python content into C and makes direct C-level API calls into the Python translator.

Python's advancement was improved to a great extent by the Python Enhancement Proposal (PEP) process. This included gathering community contribution on issues and recording Python structure decisions. Python coding style is canvassed in PEP 8. Outstanding PEPs are assessed and remarked on by the Python community and the controlling council.

Improvement of the language compares with the advancement of the CPython reference usage. The mailing list, Python-dev, is the essential discussion for the language's advancement. Explicit issues are talked about in the Roundup bug tracker kept up at Python.org. Development initially occurred on a self-facilitated source-code storehouse running Mercurial, until Python moved to GitHub in January 2017.

CPython's open discharges come in three kinds, recognized by which part of the adaptation number is augmented.

Backward-contrary variants is where code is required to break and should be physically ported. The initial segment of the adaptation number is increased. These discharges happen rarely—for instance, adaptation 3.0 was discharged eight years after 2.0.

Major or "feature" discharges are like clockwork, and include new features. The second piece of the form number is increased. Each significant variant is upheld by bug fixes for quite a long while after its release.

Bug-fix discharges, which present no new includes, happen at regular intervals and are made when an adequate number of bugs have been fixed upstream since the last discharge. Security vulnerabilities are, likewise fixed, in these discharges. The third and last piece of the form number is incremented.

Numerous **alpha and beta discharge** up-and-comers are additionally discharged as sneak peeks, and for testing before conclusive discharges. Even though there is an unpleasant timetable for each discharge, they are frequently deferred if the code isn't prepared. Python's advancement group screens the condition of the code by running a huge unit test suite during improvement, and utilizing the BuildBot ceaseless combination system. The community of Python engineers has additionally contributed over 86,000 programming modules. The real scholastic Conference on Python is PyCon. There are likewise extraordinary Python coaching programs, for example, Pyladies.

1.4 Python Applications

Python is known for its broadly useful nature that makes it relevant in practically every space of programming advancement. Python can be used in a plethora of ways for improvement; there are specifying application territories where Python can be applied.

Web-Applications

We can utilize Python to create web applications. It gives libraries to deal with web conventions, for example, HTML and XML, JSON, email handling, demand, beautiful soup, Feedparser, and so on. Additionally, it there is Frameworks. For example, Django, Pyramid, Flask, and so on to structure and develop electronic applications. Some significant improvements are PythonWikiEngines, PythonBlogSoftware, and so on.

Desktop GUI Applications

Python gives a Tk-GUI library to create UI in Python based application. Another valuable toolbox includeds wxWidgets, Kivy, and is useable on a few stages. The Kivy is well known for comp sing multitouch applications.

Software Development

Python is useful for programming advanced processes. It functions as a help language and can be utilized for fabricating control and the board, testing, and so forth.

Scientific and Numeric

Python is mainstream and generally utilized in logical and numeric figuring. Some helpful libraries and bundles are SciPy, Pandas, IPython, and so forth. SciPy is a library used for the collection of bundles of designing, science, and arithmetic.

Business Applications

Python is utilized to manufacture business applications, like ERP and online business frameworks. Tryton is an abnormal state application stage.

Console Based Application

It can be utilized for support-based applications. For instance: IPython.

Audio or Video-based Applications

Python is great for playing out various assignments and can be utilized to create media applications. Some of the genuine applications are TimPlayer, cplay, and so on.

3D CAD Applications

To make CAD application, Fandango is a genuine application that gives full highlights of CAD.

Enterprise Applications

Python can be utilized to make applications that can be utilized inside an Enterprise or an Organization. Some ongoing applications are OpenERP, Tryton, Picalo, etc.

Applications for Images

Utilizing Python, a few applications can be created for a picture. Various applications include VPython, Gogh and imgSeek.

1.5 Why Python to Conduct Data Analysis

Different programming languages can be utilized for data science (for example SQL, Java, Matlab, SAS, R and some more), yet Python is the most favored by data researchers among the various programming languages in this rundown. Python has some exceptional features including:

- Python is solid and basic with the goal that it is anything but difficult to gain proficiency in the language. You don't have to stress over its linguistic structure on the off chance that you are an amateur. Its syntax is similar to English writing; that's why it is an easy to use the programming language.

- Python supports almost all platforms, like Windows, Mac, and Linux.

- It has multiple data structures with which complex calculations can easily be simplified.

- Python is an open-source programming language that enables the data scientists to get pre-defined libraries and codes to perform their tasks.

- Python can perform data visualization, data investigation, and data control.

- Python serves different ground-breaking libraries for algorithms and logical calculations. Different complex logical figuring and AI calculations can be performed utilizing this language effectively in a moderately basic sentence structure.

1.6 Python Version List

Python programming language is updated constantly with new components and supports.

Below is the list of Python versions with its released date is given:

Python Version	Released Date
Python 1.0	January 1994
Python 1.5	December 31, 1997
Python 1.6	September 5, 2000
Python 2.0	October 16, 2000
Python 2.1	April 17, 2001
Python 2.2	December 21, 2001
Python 2.3	July 29, 2003
Python 2.4	November 30, 2004
Python 2.5	September 19, 2006
Python 2.6	October 1, 2008
Python 2.7	July 3, 2010
Python 3.0	December 3, 2008
Python 3.1	June 27, 2009
Python 3.2	February 20,2011
Python 3.3	September 29, 2012
Python 3.4	March 16, 2014
Python 3.5	September 13, 2015
Python 3.6	December 23, 2016
Python 3.7	June 27, 2018

1.7 How to Install Python

Python is easily available on internet and can be downloaded from various websites. A few examples for installation of Python are as follows:

Installation on Windows

Open the link https://www.Python.org/downloads/ in order to download the latest release of Python. In this method, a window will open with different versions of Python, and you can install Python 3.6.7.

After selecting that, double-click the executable file, which is downloaded. A window will open.

Select Customize installation and proceed.

Now a window will depict all the optional features. All the features needed to be installed and are checked by default.

Click next to continue.

Window pops-up show advanced options. Check all of the required options and click next.

Then we can to install Python-3.6.7.

Now, let's run Python on the command prompt. Write the command Python; it may show error. This is because the path has not been set.

In order to set the path of Python, right-click on "My PC" and select Properties → select Advanced → select Environment Variables.

New Path in the user variable section will be added

Write PATH as the variable name and set the path to the installation directory of Python.

When the path is set, we can now run Python on our local system. Restart CMD, and type Python again. Finally, Python interpreter will be opened where we can execute the Python statements.

The least demanding approach to introduce things in the Command line is utilizing the apt-get application's install functionality. You need to type apt-get install. If the extra exists, apt-get will discover and submit it. Unfortunately, the version of apt-get on your server isn't the latest one, so as an initial step, update it with this Command:

sudo apt-get update

Through this command, you can update the version and can run the installation process.

Chapter 2

Python Functions and File Handling

Python functions and file handling are the most important part of Python for data science. Without using these functionalities, no data scientist can achieve results. They are easy to understand codes that can be called up anywhere in the main Python code.

2.1 Functions in Python

Python functions are highly useful small block of code that can be called to run a specific function. They are used in programs to perform special roles. Basically, they are unique statements that are enclosed by {}. They can be called as many times as required.

Advantage of Python functions

Here are some major advantages of Python functions:

- They avoid repetition of code. With a single statement, the whole function can be called. It saves a lot of time.

- Their reusability is a very attractive feature. It can be called a number of times in a program.

- Through these functions, a large program can be divided into multiple functions. It enhances the usage.

Functions of Python

There are many functions in Python programming language. They can be called from interpreter package to use in any program. Without these functions, this language has no attraction for the software community. Nowadays, they are being used across the world to perform major programming tasks related to data science and other projects.

The abs() Function in Python

This function is mainly for numeric values. It gives back an absolute value when you enter any integer. It is specifically for getting absolute values against one single argument. Here are some examples of absolute numbers to understand the concept.

For Example

```
# int number
Int= -25
Print(' abs value of -25 is', abs(int)
#float number
Float= -55
Print('abs value of -55', abs(float)
```

Result/ Output:

abs value of -25 is: 25
abs value of -55 is: 55
These results are defining 'how function' works.

The bin() Function in Python

This function, bin(), returns the binary results of an integer. The binary output has prefix 0b at the start of value.

For Example

Let's evaluate this function from this syntax elaboration of function.

> *c=20*
> *d= bin(a)*
> *print(d)*
> *Output:*
> *0b2020*

The bool() Function in Python

This function gives an output in Boolean value by using truth testing methods. It is a very important built-in function of Python. If there is any value input, the result is true, otherwise it prints false.

For Example

Let's evaluate this function from this syntax elaboration of function.

> *X1=[5]*
> *Print(x1, 'is',bool(x1))*
> *x1= No-value*
> *Print(x1, 'is',bool(x1))*

Result/ Output:

> *[5] is True*
> *No-value is False*
> *These results are defining 'how function' works.*

The bytes() Function in Python

The bytes() function is very useful to get object in bytes. It belongs to the command byte-array. Mostly, Python programming experts get help by generating objects through this command.

For Example

Let's evaluate this function from this syntax elaboration of function.

> *String= "Hi Python."*
> *Array= bytes(String, 'utf-8')*
> *Print(Array)*

Results:

> *' Hi Python.'*
> *These results are defining 'how function' works.*

The callable() Function

This function investigates and shows up 'true' when objects seems callable, otherwise it shows False. This function saves time by notifying the user about the availability of an object with s single command.

For Example

Let's evaluate this function from this syntax elaboration of function.

> *C= 12*
> *Print(callable(C))*

Result/ Output:

> *False*
> *These results are defining 'how function' works.*

The compile() Function in Python

The compile() works on source code by using the compilers of Python, and ultimately generates an object with code. Later, we execute this code by using the function exec() in the same program.

For Example

Let's evaluate this function from this syntax elaboration of function.

```
Code_str= c=10\n d=15\n print("sum=",c+d)'
Code=compile(code_str, "sum.py",'exec')
Print(type(code))
Exec(code)
Exec(c)
```

Output:

```
sum = 25
These results are defining 'how function' works.
```

The exec() Function in Python

The exec() function has extra importance within the built-in functions of Python. It runs the programs of Python and produces results. Without this function, Python programs can't execute.

For Example

Let's evaluate this function from this syntax elaboration of function.

```
b = 12
exec('print(b==12)')
exec('print(b+4)')
```

True

16

These results are defining 'how function' works.

The sum() Function in Python

When we work with arithmetic operations by using numerical data, the Sum() function becomes inevitable. We use this function to perform addition of values available in the list.

For Example

Let's evaluate this function from this syntax elaboration of function.

x = sum([2, 5,4])

print(x)

x= sum([4, 2, 4], 10)

print(x)

Output:

11

20

These results are defining 'how function' works.

The any() Function in Python

The any() function of Python gives the result or output in Boolean value, which may be true or false. It prints true when there is any value 'true' in the list. But if there is not any value true, it gives a false. It is also a very useful function for data scientist who work on big data projects.

For Example

Let's evaluate this function from this syntax elaboration of function.

```
5=[4, False,9]
Print(any(5))
5=[]
Print(any(5))
```

Result:

True

False

These results are defining 'how function' works.

The ascii() Function in Python

The ascii() function has an important role in Python data science programming. The output value of this function is always 'string'. It doesn't print other ascii characters.

For Example

Let's evaluate this function from this syntax elaboration of function.

```
nT= 'Have a good day'
print(ascii(nT))
oT= 'Have a good day'
print(ascii(oT))
print('Have\xf6n a good day')
```

'Have a good day'

'Have\xf6n a good day'

'Have a good day'

These results are defining 'how function' works.

The bytearray() Function in Python

The bytearray function plays an integral role in Python programming. To create an object, this command helps users or software professionals without wasting time.

For Example

Let's evaluate this function from this syntax elaboration of function.

String1= "Python Data Science"

#string1 with encode 'utf-8'

Array1= bytearray(string, 'utf-8')

Print(array1)

Result:

bytearray(b'Python Data Science')

These results are defining 'how function' works.

The eval() Function in Python

The eval() function has an additional role in Python programming. This function executes itself in a running program, helping the code manager to get work done quickly.

For Example

Let's evaluate this function from this syntax elaboration of function.

$Y= 6$
Print(eval('Y+1')

Output:

7

These results are defining 'how function' works.

The format() Function of Python

This format() function of Python makes the coding easier for every programmer. By formatting the values and other given data, it saves the time of the coding master.

For Example

Let's evaluate this function from this syntax elaboration of function.

 # d, f and b are a type
 # integer
print(format(515, "d"))
 # float arguments
print(format(515.7898, "f"))
 # binary format
print(format(15, "b"))

Result/Output:

245
363.790
35
These results are defining 'how function' works.

The frozenset() Funcion of Python

The frozenset() function provides a changeable frozen-set object. This is a very useful function of Python.

For Example

Let's evaluate this function from this syntax elaboration of function.

> *letter = ('j', 'k', 'l', 'm', 'p')*
> *frozSet = frozenset(letter)*
> *print('Frozen set:', frozSet)*
> *print('set with no value:',Frozenset())*

Outcome:

> *Frozen set: ({'k', 'p', 'j', 'm', 'l'})*
> *Set with no val: frozenset()*

> *These results are defining 'how function' works.*

The getattr() Function of Python

This function has a very important role in Python language. With this command, the user is able to get object's attribute. Software programmers use this function to assign names to the objects.

For Example:

Let's evaluate this function from this syntax elaboration of function.

> *class Details:*
> *age = 21*
> *name = "john"*
> *detail = Details()*

```
print('age:', getattr(detail, "age"))
print('age:', detail.age)
```

Result/ Output:

age: 21
age: 21
These results are defining 'how function' works.

The globals() Function of Python

This function enables the user to get the table of global symbols (data structure) with all the information of variables and methods. It is a mandatory function to have all the symbols ready to use in any Python program. Let's see into this example to understand this function:

Example:

Let's evaluate this function from this syntax elaboration of function.

```
Id = 25
globals()['Id'] = 25
print(' My id :', Id)
```

Result:

My id : 25
These results are defining 'how function' works.

The hasattr() Function of Python

This function is based on Boolean returns: true and false.

For Example

Let's evaluate this function from this syntax elaboration of function.

```
l = [0, False, 5]
print(any(l))
l = []
print(any(l))
```

Results:

True

False

These results are defining 'how function' works.

The iter() Function of Python

This function is commonly used as it plays with the values inside an object list. It prints the values in a list one by one.

For Example

Let's evaluate this function from this syntax elaboration of function.

```
# list of numbers
list = [6,7,8,9,}

listIter = iter(list)
# prints '6'
print(next(listIter))
```

```
# prints '7'
print(next(listIter))

# prints '8'
print(next(listIter))
# prints '9'
print(next(listIter))
```

Result/Output:

6

7

8

9

These results are defining 'how function' works.

The len() Function of Python

It is a simple, but extremely important function of Python programming. The users or programmers measure the length of items by using this function.

For Example

Let's evaluate this function from this syntax elaboration of function.

```
stringX = 'Data'
print(len(stringX))
Result:
4
```
These results are defining 'how function' works.

The list() Function of Python

This function is one of the most commonly used functions which generates a complete list of a set of given instructions.

For Example

Let's evaluate this function from this syntax elaboration of function.

```
print(list())
#for empty list
# string
String = 'abcde'
print(list(String))
# tuple
Tuple = (1,2,3,4,5)
print(list(Tuple))
# list
List = [1,2,3,4,5]
print(list(List))
```

The locals() Function of Python

It provides a Boolean result against the input (True or False). It takes two inputs and returns true or false according to the defined program.

For Example

Let's evaluate this function from this syntax elaboration of function.

```
def localsJunior():
return locals()
def localstSenior():
```

Senior = True

return locals()

print('localsNoAutority:', localsJunior())

print('localsHighAuthority:', localsSenior())

Result:

localsJunior: {}

localsSenior: {'present': True}

These results are defining 'how function' works.

The map() Function of Python

This function is really important, as it provides an item's list processed under this function.

For Example

Let's evaluate this function from this syntax elaboration of function.

def calculateAddition(n):

return n+n

numbers = (1, 2, 3, 4)

result = map(calculateAddition, numbers)

print(result)

 # converting map object to set

numbersAddition = set(result)

print(numbersAddition)

Result / Output:

<map object at 0x7fb04a6bec18>

These results are defining 'how function' works.

The delattr() Function in Python

This function is more important than the addition function. On every step, a developer or user needs to delete attributes from class and shows errors on calling the same attribute.

For Example

Let's evaluate this function from this syntax elaboration of function.

> *Class Employee:*
> *ID= 21*
> *Name= "John"*
> *Email= "john@xyz "*
>
> *Def getinfo(self):*
> *Print(self.id, self.name, self.email)*
> *E=employee()*
> *e.getinfo()*
> *delattrib(Employee, 'Job Description')*
> *e.getinfo()*

Result / Output:

> *21 John John@xyz*
> *These results are defining 'how function' works.*

The divmod() Function in Python

This function performs a numerical operation on given values. The arguments that this function uses are numeric values. In all numeric operations, this function is frequently used and preferred.

For Example

Let's evaluate this function from this syntax elaboration of function.

$X = divmod(30,5)$
print(X)

Result/ Output:

(6, 0)
These results are defining 'how function' works.

The enumerate() Function of Python

This function is based on sequence of index numbers. Through using element's sequence and index, it generates an object with numerical values.

For Example

Let's evaluate this function from this syntax elaboration of function.

$Y = enumerate([4,5,6])$
print(Y)
print(list(Y))

Result/ Output:

[(0, 4), (1, 5), (2, 6)]
These results are defining 'how function' works.

The dict() Function of Python

It returns a dictionary. This function generates three types of dictionary:

Empty Dictionary: When there is no argument passed.

Identical Key-value pair Dictionary: When there is a potential argument given.

Keyword and Value added Dictionary: When there is a keyword argument.

For Example

Let's evaluate this function from this syntax elaboration of function.

```
X = dict()
Y = dict(c=4,d=5)
print(result)
print(result2)
```

Result/ Output:

```
{} #empty dictionary
{'c': 4, 'd':5} #dictionary with values
These results are defining 'how function' works.
```

The filter() Function of Python

It is used for the filtration of values by providing two arguments: function and iterable. In case of (none) function, it returns only TRUE.

For Example

Let's evaluate this function from this syntax elaboration of function.

> *def filterdata(y):*
> *if y>4:*
> *return y*
> *Result = filter(filterdata,(1,2,7))*
> *print(list(Result))*

Result/ Output:

> *[7]*
> *These results are defining 'how function' works.*

The hash() Function of Python

It generates the numeric value through hash algorithm. These values may be integers used for comparison of dictionary keys.

For Example

Let's evaluate this function from this syntax elaboration of function.

> *X = hash(35)*
> *Y = hash(35.6)*
> *print(X)*
> *print(Y)*

Output:

> *35*
> *756783388388221*
> *These results are defining 'how function' works.*

The help() Function of Python

It calls help to assist the process of object passage. Through an additional parameter, this function shares the help data with you.

For Example

Let's evaluate this function from this syntax elaboration of function.

> *Information = help()*
> *print(Information)*

Output:

> *Help Centre!*
> *These results are defining 'how function' works.*

The min() Function of Python

This function helps get the smallest or basic element by taking two arguments as input: elements list and Key.

For Example

Let's evaluate this function from this syntax elaboration of function.

> *X = min(2100,221,225)*
> *Y = min(1000.25,2025.35,5625.36,10052.50)*
> *print(X)*
> *print(Y)*

Output:

> *221*
> *1000.25*
> *These results are defining 'how function' works.*

The set() Function of Python

It generates an object by using iterable object. This function of Python programming is considered the base of programs.

For Example

Let's evaluate this function from this syntax elaboration of function.

```
b = set('25')
c= set('Python')
print(b)
print(c)
```

Output:

{'2', '5'}
{'y', 'o', 't', 'h',',' 'p', 'n'}
These results are defining 'how function' works.

The hex() Function of Python

It converts the integer argument into hexadecimal string value. This function makes the conversion easy for all the programmers, software engineers and professional IT experts.

For Example

Let's evaluate this function from this syntax elaboration of function.

```
a = hex(4)
b= hex(140)
print(a)
print(b)
```

    0x2

    0x70

    These results are defining 'how function' works.

The id() Function of Python

This function generates an identity (integer) by using an argument. Let's try to understand this concept through an example

Example:

Let's evaluate this function from this syntax elaboration of function.

    X = id("Python")

    Y = id(1500)

    Z= id([95,236,92,3225])

    print(X)

    print(Y)

    print(Z)

Result/Output:

    59696771728

    66864236539

    19945047867

    These results are defining 'how function' works.

The setattr() Function of Python

It helps in setting of an attribute of an object. It takes different values and after application of function, it gives nothing.

For Example:

Let's evaluate this function from this syntax elaboration of function.

> *RN = 0   #RN- roll number*
> *Name = ""*
> *def_init_(my, RN, Name):*
> *my.RN = RN*
> *self.Name = Name*
> *X= Student(121,"John")*
> *print(X.RN)*
> *print(X.Name)*
> *#print(X.email) product error*
> *setattr(X, 'email','John@abc.com') # adding new attribute*
> *print(X.email)*

Output:

> *121*
> *John*
> john@abc.com
> *These results are defining 'how function' works.*

The slice() Function of Python

This function gives slice from a group of elements. Initially it takes a single argument, but a second function requires three arguments to proceed.

Let's evaluate this function from this syntax elaboration of function.

> *X = slice(7)*
> *Y = slice(0,7,3)*
> *print(X)*
> *print(Y)*

The sorted() Function of Python

It is for the sorting of elements in ascending order. To proceed, this function normally uses four values.

For Example

Let's evaluate this function from this syntax elaboration of function.

X = "javapoint"

Y = sorted(X) # sorting string

print(Y)

The next() Function of Python

This function enables you to get the next element from the given group. Through two arguments, this function produces a single element.

For Example:

Let's evaluate this function from this syntax elaboration of function.

> *X = iter([128, 16, 42])*

Y= next(X)

print(Y)

Y = next(X)

print(Y)

Y= next(X)

print(Y)

#X is number

#Y is item

Result/ Output:

128

16

42

These results are defining 'how function' works.

The input() Function of Python

This function is for taking instructions from the programmer or software developer or user. After getting information, it converts the value into program required data format.

For Example:

Let's evaluate this function from this syntax elaboration of function.

Value = input("Please insert value: ")

print("You entered:",Value)

Result/ Output:

Please Insert value:22

You entered: 22

These results are defining 'how function' works.

The int() Function of Python

This function is designed to get integers; normally users use it to convert strings and other data structures into specified integer value.

For Example:

Let's evaluate this function from this syntax elaboration of function.

```
a = int(15) # integer
b = int(15.52) # float
c = int('15') # string
print("Int val:",a, b, c)
```

Result/ Output:

Int val : 15 15 15

These results are defining 'how function' works.

The pow() Function of Python

It computes number power to define it for some specific results needed for the project or program. It is really an important function to carry out many algebraic solutions.

For Example:

Let's evaluate this function from this syntax elaboration of function.

```
#Positive a, Positive b (a**b)
print(pow(2, 3))

# Negative a, Positive b
print(pow(-2, 3))
```

 # Positive a, Negative b (x**-y)

print(pow(2, -3))

 # Negative a, Negative b

print(pow(-2, -3))

Result/ Output:

8

8

These results are defining 'how function' works.

The print() Function of Python

It gives the print of the object on screen.

For Example

Let's evaluate this function from this syntax elaboration of function.

Print("Python Data Science")

a = 7

print("a =", a)

b = a

print('a =', a, '= b')

Results / Output:

Python Data Science

a = 7

a = 7 = b

These results are defining 'how function' works.

The range() Function of Python

It provides the sequence: begins at 0 normally and it increases by 1 and stops on a specific number.

For Example:

Let's evaluate this function from this syntax elaboration of function.

```
print(list(range(9,12)))
range(start, stop)
```

Result/ Output:

```
[10,11]
```
These results are defining 'how function' works.

The reversed() Function of Python

It returns the reverse sequence of a given sequence.

For Example:

```
String = 'Python'
print(list(reversed(String)))

Tuple = ('J', 'a', 'v', 'a')
print(list(reversed(Tuple)))

Range = range(10, 12)
print(list(reversed(Range)))

List = [1, 2, 7, 5]
print(list(reversed(List)))
```

['n', 'o', 'h', 't', 'y','P']

These results are defining 'how function' works.

The round() Function of Python

This function is mostly used when there are decimals in the list of numbers. Let's look at this example to understand this function.

For Example:

Let's evaluate this function from this syntax elaboration of function.

> *print(round(8))*
> *print(round(10.4))*
> *print(round(6.6))*

Result/ Output:

> *8*
> *10*
> *7*

These results are defining 'how function' works.

The str() Function of Python

It transforms any value into string. This conversion function helps user to get things done quickly.

For Example:

Let's evaluate this function from this syntax elaboration of function.

> *str('6')*

'6'

These results are defining 'how function' works.

The tuple() Function of Python

It generates an object through this function. This function allows users to get their required object by writing a simple syntax.

For Example:

Let's evaluate this function from this syntax elaboration of function.

a = tuple()
print('a=', a)
b = tuple([2, 8, 10])
print('b=', b)
a = tuple('Python')
print('a=',a)
a = tuple({4: 'four', 5: 'five'})
print('a=',a)

Result/ Output:

a= ()
b= (2, 8, 10)
a= ('P', 'y', 't', 'h','o','n')
a= (4, 5)
These results are defining 'how function' works.

The type() function of Python

This function is normally applied to understand the type. With three arguments, the type function gives an object.

For Example:

Let's evaluate this function from this syntax elaboration of function.

> *X = [4, 5]   #LIST*
> *print(type(X))*
> *Y = {4: 'four', 5: 'five'} #Dictionary*
> *print(type(Y))*
>
> *class Python:*
> *a = 0*
>
> *InstanceOfPython = Python()*
> *print(type(InstanceOfPython))*

Result/ Output:

> *<class 'X'>*
> *<class 'Y'>*
> *<class '__main__.Python'>*
> *These results are defining 'how function' works.*

The vars() function of Python

It returns the attribute that belongs to the dictionary. It is an important function of Python.

Let's evaluate this function from this syntax elaboration of function.

```
class Python:
def _init_(my, a = 7, b = 9):
my.a = a
my.b = b
InstanceOfPython = Python()
print(vars(InstanceOfPython))
```

Result/ Output:

{'b': 9, 'a': 7}

These results are defining 'how function' works.

The zip() Function of Python

It gives an object having the same index with several containers. Through this function, results can be produced in zip form.

For Example:

Let's evaluate this function from this syntax elaboration of function.

```
numericalList = [4,5, 6]
stringList = ['four', 'five', 'six']
X = zip()
XList = list(X)
print(XList)

X= zip(numberList, stringList)

XSet = set(result)
print(XSet)
```

2.2 File Handling of Python

Python also supports files and enables clients to deal with the reading and writing of documents, alongside numerous methods to deal with the available file documents. The idea of file management has extended over different languages. This programming language has multiple unique features and functions to take care of files. It distinguishes other high-level programming languages on the basis of the structural organization of file management. It is an easy to learn and implement the coding module in Python. We should begin with Reading and Writing files.

The linguistic structure is: open(filename, mode). Here is a list of some commands to open the file.

File Opening Using Function open()

We utilize open () function for reading and writing. As stated above, it restores an object in file format. We utilize open() work alongside two contentions that acknowledge file management.

Syntax for file opening

Object File= open(<name>, <mode>, <buffering>)

For Closing of flie: close() function of Pyhton

After the completion of the program, the user must close the file by using Python script: close(). It secures the file from external threats and manipulation of functionalities.

Syntax: file.close()

Example:

Fileabc=open("file.txt","r")
if fileabc:
print("opened successfully")
fileabc.close()

Chapter 3

Variables, Operators, and Data Types of Python

Theree are some really very important concepts in Python that are considered as basic building blocks of this high-level programming language. We use them to program our projects and get the required results through their functionalities. Data types are essential concepts, and no one can understand the Python programming without having command over these basic concepts. We will discuss the important variables, operators, and data types of Python programming language.

3.1 Variables of Python

Variable, a name identifier, is a term that is used to imply memory zone. In Python, we don't need to decide the kind of factor, since Python infers language and is astute enough to understand variable sort.

In any case, we need a letter or an underscore. Use lowercase letters for the variable names. Mallet and sledge are two exceptional elements.

Naming of Identifier

Factors are the situation of identifiers. An identifier is used to perceive the literals used in the program. The standards to name an identifier are given below.

- The essential character of the variable must be a letter or underscore (_).

- Every one of the characters beside the essential character may be a letter arranged by lower-case(a-z), promoted (A-Z), underscored, or a digit (0-9).

- The identifier name must not contain any void zone, or extraordinary characters (Ex: ! @, #, %, ^, and, *).

- The identifier name must not resemble any catchphrase portrayed in Python syntax.

- They are case sensitive. For example, my name, and My name isn't recognized as the same.

- Instances of considerable identifiers: a123, _n, n_9, etc.

- Instances of invalid identifiers: 1a, n%4, n 9, etc.

Multiple Assignments

Python enables doling out an incentive to numerous variables in a solitary explanation, which is otherwise called multiple assignments. It can be applied in two different ways: either by doling out a solitary incentive to various variables, or relegating various qualities to numerous variables.

Example:

```
a=b=c=60
print
print z
```

Output:

```
>>>
60
60
60
>>>
```

Example:

```
x,y,z=21,25,45
print x
print y
print z
```

Output:

```
>>>
21
25
45
>>>
```

3.2 Operators in Python

Operator is portrayed as a symbolic representation of a function that does a particular activity between two operands to achieve a specific result. Operators are viewed as the mainstays of a program in which the rationale is worked in an individual programming language. Assortment of operators given by Python is portrayed as pursues. Here are some commonly used operators to perform special operations:

- Arithmetic operators
- Comparison operators
- Assignment Operators
- Logical Operators
- Bitwise Operators
- Membership Operators
- Identity Operators

Arithmetic operators

These operators are used for specific arithmetic operations to get results. Two operands are taken, and activity through an operator is performed resulting in some desired value.

Here is some very important arithmetic operators used in Python.

Detailed Description

ADDITION +

It is to perform addition or sum function between two operands. E.g. if x = 25, y = 15 => x+y = 40

SUBTRACTION -

It subtracts 2nd operand from the 1st operand. E.g. if x = 40, y = 10 => x - y = 30

DIVISION /

It divides the 1st operand by 2nd operand, and gives quotient. e.g. if x = 20, y = 2 => x/y = 10

MULTIPLICATION *

It performs a multiplication operation. For example, if x = 30, y = 10 => x * y = 300

REMAINDER %

It performs the operation of division and gets remainder. For example, if x=30, y=10, x/y=0

Comparison operator in Python

They are used to compare two operands, and returns Boolean (TRUE or FALSE) respectively.

Description of Python Comparison Operators

==

True: when the values are equal

!=

True: When the values are unequal.

<=

True: When 1st operand is smaller than or equal to the second operand.

>=

True: When 1st operand is greater than or equal to the second operand.

<>

True: when the values are not equal.

>

True: when 1st operand is greater than 2nd Operand.

<

True: when 1st operand is less than the 2nd operand.

Assignment operators in Python

In Python, assignment operators are utilized to assign the value of the right expression to the left operand.

Description of Python's Assignment Operators

=

Normally it assigns value of the right expression to the left operand.

+=

It builds the estimation of the left operand by the estimation of the correct operand and appoints the altered an incentive back to left operand. For instance, if a = 10, b = 20 => a+ = b will be equivalent to a = a+ b and hence, a = 30.

-=

It diminishes the estimation of the left operand by the estimation of the correct operand and doles out the changed incentive back to left operand. For instance, if a = 20, b = 10 => a-= b will be equivalent to a = a-b and in this way, a = 10.

*=

It increases the estimation of the left operand by the estimation of the correct operand and appoints the altered incentive back to left operand. For instance, if a = 10, b = 20 => a* = b will be equivalent to a = a* b and subsequently, a = 200.

%=

Divides the estimation of the left operand by that of the correct operand and appoints the update back to the left operand. For instance, if a = 20, b = 10 => a % = b will be equivalent to a = a % b and thusly, a = 0.

Logical Operators in Python

They are used to evaluate the expression to reach a decision. They are very helpful to write any logic in an understandable way. Here is the list of logical operators with a brief description to build a better understanding of these operators in Python.

Logical Operator Description

and

True Condition: If an expression "a" is true, and another expression "b" is true as well, then the result will be true.

For example, a → true, b → true => a and b → true.

or

True Condition: If an expression "a" is true, and another expression "b" is false, then the result will be true.

For example, a → true, b → false => a or b → true.

3.3 Python Data Types

Factors can hold estimations of various data types. Python is a progressively composed language, therefore, we need not characterize the kind of variable while pronouncing it. The interpreter ties the incentive with its sort.

Python enables us to check the sort of variable utilized in the program. Python provides us the type () work which returns the kind of the variable passed.

Consider the accompanying guide to characterize the estimations of various data types and checking its sort.

Example:

```
a=15
b="Hi Python"
c = 15.5
print(type(a));
print(type(b));
print(type(c));
```

Output:

```
<type 'int'>
<type 'str'>
<type 'float'>
```

Standard data types

Variable can withstand various kinds of qualities. For instance, an individual's name must be put away as a string, while its id must be put away as a whole number.

Python gives different standard data types that characterize the capacity technique on every one of them. The data types characterized in Python are given below.

- Numbers
- String
- List
- Tuple
- Dictionary

Now we will explain each data type with examples.

Numbers

Number stores numeric values. Python generated number objects whenever a number is given to a variable. For example:

1. a = 3 , b = 5 #a and b are number objects

Four different types of numeric data are supported by Python.

int (signed integers like 12, 22, 39, etc.)

long (long integers used for a relatively higher range of values like 908800L, -0x19292L, etc.)

float (float is used to store floating-point like 1.7, 9.1902, 151.2, etc.)

Complex (complex numbers like 12.14j, 2.0 + 12.3j, etc.)

Python allows to use a lower-case L to be used with long integers. But we must ensure that always an upper-case L is used for clarity.

A complex number consists of an ordered pair, i.e., a + ib, where a and b denote the real and imaginary parts respectively).

String

String can be described as the sequence of characters that are represented in the quotation marks. Also, single, double, or triple quotes can be used to define a string.

String handling is a simple, and clear task, since there are many in-built functions and operators provided in Python.

For string handling, the operator + is used to concatenate two strings as the operation "hello"+" Mr. Davir" returns "hello Mr. David".

The operator * is known as a repetition operator as the operation "Python" *2 returns "Python Python ".

String handling in Python is illustrated in following example

Example:

```
string1 = 'hello Mr. David'
string2 = ' how are you'
print (string1[0:2]) #printing first two character using slice operator
print (string1[4]) #printing 4th character of the string
print (string1*2) #printing the string twice
print (string1 + str2) #printing the concatenation of string1 and string2
```

Output:

```
he
o
hello Mr. David hello Mr. David
hello Mr. David how are you
```

String Operators

+

Operator 'Addition' is used to join the strings in a program.

*

Operator with symbol 'Multiplication' is for the generation of multiple copies of the same string to perform a function.

[]

Slice Operator makes available the sub-strings of a specified string.

[:]

This range slice operator performs function of getting characters.

In

This membership operator returns value against the presence of specific sub-string in the main string.

%

It is employed to perform string formatting.

Lists

Lists are identical to arrays in C. But the list can contain data of various types. The stored items in the list are separated with a comma (,) and enclosed within square brackets [].

Slice [:] operators can be employed for accessing the list's. The concatenation operator (+) and repetition operator (*) work with the list in a similar way as they were working with the strings.

Example:

```
l = [1.5, "Hi", "Python", 2]
print (l[3:]);
print (l[0:2]);
print (l);
print (l + l);
print (l * 3);
```

Output:

```
[2]
[1.5, 'Hi']
[1.5, 'Hi', 'Python', 2]
[1.5, 'Hi', 'Python', 2, 1.5, 'Hi', 'Python', 2]
[1.5, 'Hi', 'Python', 2, 1.5, 'Hi', 'Python', 2, 1.5, 'Hi', 'Python', 2]
```

Python List Built-in Functions Description

Built-in function	Description
len(list):	length of the list.
max(list):	maximum element of the list.
min(list):	minimum element of the list.
cmp(list1, list2):	comparing the elements of both the lists.
list(seq):	sequence to the list.

Tuple

It is identical to the list in a lot of ways. Similar to lists, tuples also possess the collection of the items of various data types. The items of the tuple are segregated with a comma (,) and enclosed in parentheses ().

A tuple can't modify the size and value of the items of a tuple.

Example:

```
t = ("Hi", "Python world", 4)
print (t[1:]);
print (t[0:1]);
print (t);
print (t + t);
print (t * 3);
print (type(t))
t[2] = "hi";
```

Output:

```
('Python world', 4)
('Hi',)
('Hi', 'Python world', 4)
('Hi', 'Python world', 4, 'Hi', 'Python world', 2)
('hi', 'Python world', 4, 'Hi', 'Python world', 4, 'Hi', 'Python world', 4)
<type 'tuple'>
Traceback (most recent call last):
File "main.py", line 8, in <module>
t[2] = "Hello";
TypeError: 'tuple' object does not support assignment
```

Chapter 4

Python Regular Expressions, Statements, Loops

Python regular expressions, statements and loops are the totality of Python programming. All of these functions, methods, statements and loops play a vital role in building an effective program for data analysis in Python. There are number of reasons behind the addition of these operation runners in the libraries of Python. Let's discuss the importance and functionalities of these programs.

4.1 Python Regular Expressions

The regular expression (regex) works to analyze the pattern in a string. There are a number of regex functionalities that can be imported to bring into use. For importing these functions, we can use the command: import re.

Here is a list of Regex Functions

Split: To split the string.

Sub: To replace the matches.

Match: Evaluates the regex pattern and returns True or False.

Findall: To restore all the matches in string

Search: To find the match in string.

4.2 Python Statements

The assignment statement is (token '=', the equals sign). This works differently than in conventional basic programming dialects, and this basic system (counting the idea of Python's form of factors) enlightens numerous different highlights of the language. So, the task in C, e.g., x = 2, means "composed variable name x gets a duplicate of numeric worth 2". The (right-hand) esteem is replicated into an assigned stockpiling area for which the (left-hand) variable name is the emblematic location. The memory apportioned to the variable is big enough (conceivably enormous) for the pronounced sort. In the most straightforward instance of Python task, utilizing a similar model, x = 2, means "(nonexclusive) name x gets a reference to a different, progressively assigned object of numeric (int) kind of significant worth 2."

- The (if) statement, which restrictively executes a square of code, alongside else and elif (a compression of else-if).

- The (for) statement emphasizes an iterable article, catching every component to a nearby factor for use by the connected square.

- The while statement executes a square of code as long as its condition is valid.

- The try statement permits special cases raised in its connected code square to be gotten and taken care of with the exception of provisos. Likewise, it guarantees that tidy up code in a long last square will consistently be run, paying little mind to how the square exits.

- The raise statement employes to raise a specified exemption or re-raise a special case.

- The class statement executes a square of code and appends its nearby namespace to a class for use in the item arranged programming.

- The def statement describes a capacity or technique.

- The pass statement fills in as a NOP. It is linguistically expected to make a vacant code square.

- The assert statement is utilized during troubleshooting to check for conditions that should apply.

- The yield statement restores an incentive from a generator work. From Python 2.5, yield is additionally an administrator. This form is utilized to actualize co-routines.

- The import statement is utilized to import modules whose capacities or factors can be utilized in the present program. There are three different ways of utilizing Import: import <module name> [as <alias>].

- The print statement was changed to the print () work in Python.

Explanation of some of the most mostly employed statements are as follows.

Python If-else statements

Decision making is a primary part of almost all the programming languages. As the name implies, decision making permits to execute a specified block of code for a specific decision. However, on validation of the particular condition, the decisions are made. Condition checking acts as the backbone of decision making. It is performed by the following statements in Python.

Statement Description

If Statement

The If statement is employed to test a specific condition. For Example, if this condition(code) is valid, the function proceeds.

If - else Statement

The if-else statement is identical to if statement except for the fact that it also gives insights and check the validity of code; either it is false or not. That's the reason, the else statement will be executed if the condition given in the if statement is false.

Nested if Statement

Nested if statements enable us to use if- else statement inside an outer if statement.

Indentation in Python

For the simplicity of programming and to accomplish straightforwardness, Python doesn't permit the utilization of enclosures for the square level code. In Python, indentation is utilized to pronounce a square. On the off chance that two statements are at a similar indentation level, at that point they are the piece of a similar square.

By and large, four spaces are given to indent the statements, which are a common measure of indentation in Python.

Indentation is the most utilized piece of the Python language, since it proclaims the square of code. Every one of the statements of one square is proposed at a similar level indentation. We will learn how genuine indentation happens in basic leadership and other stuff in Python.

The if statement

The (if) statement is utilized to test a specific condition and if the condition is valid, it executes a code known as if block. The condition (if) statement can be any substantial coherent articulation that can be either assessed to genuine or false.

Syntax is as follows

> *if expression:*
> *statement*

Example:

> *num = int(input("enter the number?"))*
> *if num%2 == 0:*
> *print("Number is even")*
> *Output:*
> *enter the number?10*
> *Number is even*

Example 2

> *a = int(input("Enter a? "));*
> *b = int(input("Enter b? "));*
> *c = int(input("Enter c? "));*
> *if a>b and a>c:*
> *print("a is largest");*

if b>a and b>c:
print("b is largest");
if c>a and c>b:
print("c is largest");

Output:

Enter a? 100
Enter b? 120
Enter c? 130
c is largest

The if-else statement

The if-else statement provides an else block joined with the if statement that is executed in the false case of the condition. When the condition is true, then the if-block is executed. Otherwise, the else-block is executed.

Syntax is as follows

if condition:
#block of statements
else:
#another block of statements (else-block)

Example:

age = int (input("Enter the age? "))
if age>=18:
print("You are eligible to vote !!");
else:
print("Sorry! you have to wait !!");

Output:
Enter your age? 90
You are eligible to vote !!

Example 2:

num = int(input("enter the number?"))
if num%2 == 0:
print("Number is even...")
else:
print("Number is odd...")

Output:

Enter the number? 10
Number is even

The elif statement

This statement helps to run multiple level of conditions. It must have if-an-if ladder to perform the program. It works only by taking up series of 'True' conditions.

Syntax is as follows

if expression 1:
 # block of statements
elif expression 2:
 # block of statements
elif expression 3:
 # block of statements
else:
 # block of statements

Python break statement

The break statement has a unique importance in Python loop programming. It shifts the execution pattern on the next lines by breaking up the loop from the previous codes. With simple syntax, it gives back control to the required loops in the same large program.

Syntax is break

Python continue Statement

This statement brings control of programing to the start of loop. It skips the rest of codes, and execution comes back to the beginning. It has an important role in skipping and executing specific conditions.

Syntax is as follows

> *#loop statements*
> *continue;*
> *#the code to be skipped*

Example 1:

> *i = 0;*
> *while i!=10:*
> *print("%d"%i);*
> *continue;*
> *i=i+1;*
> *Output:*
> *infinite loop*

Example 2:

```
x=1; #initializing a local variable
#starting a loop from 10 to 20
for x in range(1,10):
if x==15:
continue;
print("%d"%i);
```

Output:

```
10
11
12
13
14
16
17
18
19
20
```

Python Pass Statement

This statement is a non-executable part of the program. It appears to justify syntax, but provides only null operation. It is sometimes used when the code is not a part of program, but written somewhere outside the program.

Syntax is as follow: Pass

Example:

For a in [1,2,3,4,5]:

if a==4:

pass

print "pass when value is",a

print a,

Output:

>>>

1 2 3 Pass when value is 4

4 5

>>>

The import statement in Python

This is the most valuable statement in Python programming language. It makes possible the access of one module's functionality to another. Without the import statement, Python can't perform up to the mark level.

Syntax of 'import statement'

import module

Example:

import doc;

first name = input("input the first name?")

doc.displayMsg(first name)

Output:

Input the first name? John
Hi John

4.3 Loops in Python

Programming is all about flow of commands and functions over and again. Most of the time, the same code has to be repeated several times to get results, which is common practice in the general programming world. To make this easy for data scientists and programmers, there are many loops that are used by professionals to save time and keep the syntax easy to understand. These loops repeat the required code multiple times with only a small block of code. In Python, these loops are necessary to build up predictive models and data analysis.

Why use loops in Python?

They are very helpful to reduce the complexity of code. Syntax of loops are very easy to understand and maintain the flow of the program. It avoids repetition of the same code and through simple loop, one can easily repeat the same code a number of times.

Here are some important loops in Python.

1. **for loop**

2. **while loop**

3. **do-while loop**

4. **Python 'for' loop**

Syntax is as follows

for iterating_var in sequence:
statement(s)

Example:

i=1;
num = int(input("Enter a number:"));
for i in range(1,11):
print("%d X %d = %d"%(num,i,num*i));

Output:

Enter a number:10
10 X 1 = 10
10 X 2 = 20
10 X 3 = 30
10 X 4 = 40
10 X 5 = 50
10 X 6 = 60
10 X 7 = 70
10 X 8 = 80
10 X 9 = 90
10 X 10 = 100

Nested for loop in Python

It is about nesting a 'for loop' inside a 'for loop' to execute it multiple times.

Syntax is as follows

for iterating_var1 in sequence:

for iterating_var2 in sequence:

#block of statements

#Other statements

Example:

n = int(input("enter number of rows"))

i,j=0,0

for i in range(0,n):

print()

for j in range(0,i+1):

print("",end="")*

Output:

Enter the number of rows? 6

*

**

***

****

*****

******

Using else statement with for loop in Python

The else statement is a fundamental part of many conditional statements. It is also used in multiple languages for the satisfaction of condition. In Python, the else statement can be executed inside a 'for loop'.

Example:

for i in range(0,8):

print(i)

else:print("Excluding break statement therefore for loop completely exhausted.");

Output:

0

1

2

3

4

5

6

7

Since there is no break, for loop completely exhausted

Example:

for i in range(0,5):

print(i)

break;

else:print("for loop is exhausted");

print("break statement is used therefore loop gets broken")

#The break statement is stopping the execution of the else statement.

Output:

0

Because break statement is employed loop is broken

Python while loop

In general, a while loop enables a part of the code to be executed as long as the given condition is true. It is usually employed in the case where the iterations' quantity is not known in advance.

The syntax is given below.

while expression:
statements

Statement expressions must be any valid Python expression concluding into true or false. The true is any non-zero value.

Example:

i=1;
while i<=12:
print(i);

Output:

1
2
3
4
5
6
7
8
9
10
11
12

Example:

```
i=1
number=0
b=9
number = int(input("Enter the number?"))
while i<=10:
print("%d X %d = %d \n"%(number,i,number*i));
  i = i+1;
```

Output:

```
Enter the number? 20
20 X 1 = 20
20 X 2 = 40
20 X 3 = 60
20 X 4 = 80
20 X 5 = 100
20 X 6 = 120
20 X 7 = 140
20 X 8 = 160
20 X 9 = 180
20 X 10 = 200
```

Infinite while loop in Python

If the condition provided in the while loop doesn't become false, the while loop will never end, and the result will be an infinite while loop. To have a True Condition, we use a non-zero value in while loop, and zero value to indicate a False Condition.

> *while (1):*
> *print("Hi! we are inside the infinite while loop");*
> *Output:*
> *Hi! we are inside the infinite while loop*
> *(infinite times)*

Example:

> *var = 1*
> *while var != 2:*
> *i = int(input("Enter the number?"))*
> *print ("Entered value is %d"%(i))*

Output:

> *Enter the number? 102*
> *Entered value is 102*
> *Enter the number? 102*
> *Entered value is 102*
> *Enter the number? 103*
> *Entered value is 103*
> *Enter the number? 103*
> *(infinite loop)*

Else with Python while loop

Python empowers the client to use the while loop with the while loop too. It executes the else square when the condition given in the while articulation turns out to be false. Like for loop, on the off chance that the while loop is broken utilizing break explanation, at that point the else square won't be executed, and it will execute the announcement present after else square.

75

Example:

```
i=1;
while i<=4:
print(i)
 i=i+1;
else:print("The while loop exhausted");
```

Output:

```
1
2
3
4
```

The while loop exhausted

Example:

```
i=1;
while i<=5:
print(i)
i=i+1;
if(i==3):
break;
else:print("The while loop exhausted");
```

Output:

```
1
2
```

Chapter 5

Python OOPs Concepts

5.1 Python OOPs Concepts

Python object-oriented programming concepts play a vital role in the software industry. It has all the concepts of object-oriented programming. There are many other languages of the same core programming family, but Python is based on OOP concepts from the very beginning. Here, a software expert has the liberty to call functions, objects, and classes to perform any programming task. This language is highly recommended for data science concepts.

Let's discuss some important parts of OOPs Python:

- Object framework- Quality and methods in Python

- Class- Collection of Objects

- Method- Capacity of an object

- Inheritance- Inherits the qualities of parent object

- Polymorphism- Multiple structures

- Data Abstraction- Central quality of a program

- Encapsulation- Code and data wrapping together

Object framework

This framework has a similar concept in programming as in real world. Any existing substance with some quality is an object. In Python, there is an everywhere object-oriented approach, and all these objects have some specific qualities and functions. Having some defined capacity, objects contain all the important information that is being used to make a comprehensive result-oriented information out of it.

Class- Group of Objects

Class is about the group of objects. These classes have elements with specific attributes. Like in real life, we define classes in programming world as well. For example, we can have a class of students, workers, officers, etc. All classes have some kind of similar traits within the class.

Syntax for Class

class Name of Class:

<statement-1>

<statement-2>

<statement-N>

Method- Capacity of an Object

Method is about the capacity of an object defined in a program. It is based on how many methods an object can have. It is frequently used in Python programming.

Inheritance- Inheriting the quality of parent Object

It is an integral part of Python programming language. In OOP, it is similar to the traditional inheritance system in human biological existence. The younger object has all the traits and methods. Through this framework, we can develop classes to use the properties of one another. It helps in getting results by using single code for every class. It also saves time and can simplify the syntax.

Polymorphism- Multiple structures

This framework is an amazing feature of object-oriented programming. It has similar meaning to its name: multiple structures. It means one assignment is completed in many different methods.

Data Abstraction- Central quality of a program

This framework has excellent features through which it gets precise information to use to execute the functionality. There is no need to run a whole program to achieve results. It takes internal commands and run functionalities. We can tag functions with some names and can call them to get the functionality.

Encapsulation- Code and data wrapping together

Encapsulated code and data are an essential part of programming. It restricts the approach and code within specified users. It is done intentionally for using it in combination and keeping it secure.

Object-oriented versus Procedure-oriented Programming languages

Object-oriented	Procedural Programming
Object-oriented programming is the critical thinking approach and utilized where calculation is finished by using objects.	Procedural programming utilizes a rundown of instructions to do calculation bit by bit.

It makes the improvement and maintenance easier.	In procedural programming, It isn't difficult to maintain the codes when the undertaking ends up extensive.
It mimics this present reality element. So true issues can be effectively settled through oops.	It doesn't reenact this present reality. It chips away at bit by bit; instructions separated into little parts called capacities.
It gives data hiding. So, it is more secure than procedural dialects. You can't access to private data from anywhere.	Procedural language doesn't give any legitimate method to data binding, so it is less secure.
Example of object-oriented programming dialects is C++, Java, .Net, Python, C#, etc.	Example of procedural dialects are: C, Fortran, Pascal, VB, and so on.

5.2 Python Class and Objects

A class is basically an assumed element that contains number of objects. It is virtual and gives meaning to us when we look at it with reference to objects and their properties. For example, assume a hospital building. It has rooms, beds, medical equipment, and so on. The hospital building is a class, and all the parts of the building are its objects.

In this area of the instructional exercise, we will talk about creating classes and objects in Python. We will also discuss how to get to a characteristic by using the class object.

Creating classes in Python

Python has a very simple syntax for crating classes. A non-technical individual can make a class by just typing simple commands.

Syntax

> *class ClassName:*
> *#statement_suite*

Consider the following guide to make a class Employee, which contains two fields as Employee id, and name.

The class likewise contains a capacity show() which is utilized to show the information of the Employee.

Example

> *class Employee:*
> *id = 10;*
> *name = "ayush"*
> *def display (self):*
> *print(self.id,self.name)*

Here, self is utilized as a source of a perspective variable which alludes to the present class object. It is consistently the main argument in the capacity definition. Be that as it may, using self is discretionary in the capacity call.

Creating an instance of the class

A class should be instantiated on the off chance that we need to utilize the class characteristics in another class. It can be instantiated by calling the class using the class name.

Example:

id number = 10;

name = "John"

print("ID number: %d \nName: %s"%(self.id,self.name))

emp = Employee()

emp.display()

Output:

ID number: 10

Name: John

5.3 Python Constructor

It is a special type of method (function) that is used to initialize the specified members in a class.

There are two types of Constructors:

- Parameterized Constructor

- Non-parameterized Constructor

Its definition is executed when we create the object of this class. Constructors verify that there are measurable resources for the object to perform a task for start-up.

Creating the constructor in Python

In Python, the method __**init**__ generated the constructor of the class. This method is used when the class is instantiated. We can pass a number of arguments at the time of making the class object, using __**init**__ definition. Every class should have a constructor, even if it is simply the default constructor.

Example:

```
class Student:
count = 0
def __init__(self):
Student.count = Student.count + 1
s1=Student()
s2=Student()
s3=Student()
print("The number of students:",Student.count)
```

Output:

The number of students: 3

Python Non-Parameterized Constructor Example:

```
class Student:

def __init__(my):
print("It is non parametrized constructor")
def show(my,name):
print("Hello",name)
y = Student()
y.show("Jack")
```

Output:

It is non parametrized constructor
Hello Jack

Parameterized Constructor Example:

```
def __init__(my, firstname):
```

```
print(" parametrized constructor")
my.firstname = name
def show(my):
print("Hello",my.firstname)
s = Student("Jack")
s.show()
```

Output:

```
parametrized constructor
Hello Jack
```

Python In-built class functions

Python has multiple in-built class functions. Let's try to understand its functionality through an example.

Example:

```
class Workers:
def __init__(my,name,age):
my.name = name;
my.age = age

W = worker("Jack",115,22)
print(getattr(W,'name'))
setattr(W,"age",24)
print(getattr(s,'age'))

delattr(s,'age')
print(s.age)
```

Output:

Jack

24

True

AttributeError:There is no attribute 'age' in Student' object.

Built-in class attributes

A class in Python also contains class attributes (built-in) which give information about the class.

Here is the list of built-in class attributes:

Attribute Description

__dict__

It is for providing the dictionary containing the information about the class namespace.

__doc__

It is to contain a string that has the class documentation.

__name__

It accesses the class name.

__module__

It accesses the module in which, this class is defined.

__bases__

It is to have a tuple.

Example:

```
def __init__(my,name,roll number,age):
my.name = name;
my.rollbumber = roll number;
m.age = age
def display_details(my):
print("Name:%s,   Roll   Number:%d,   age:%d"%(my.name,my.roll
number))
Y = Student("Jack",10,17)
print(y.__doc__)
print(y.__dict__)
print(y.__module_)
```

Output:

```
None
{'name': 'Jack', 'Roll number': 10, 'age': 17}
__main__
```

5.4 Python Inheritance

Python inheritance is a very unique feature of the programming language. It improves the usability of the program and development. In this framework, a child class can access the qualities and functionalities of parent class.

Syntax

```
class derived-class(base class):
<class-suite>
```

Consider the following syntax.

Syntax

> *class derive-class(<base class 1>, <base class 2>, ...*
> *<base class n>):*
> *<class - suite>*

Example:

> *class Animal:*
> *def speak(self):*
> *print("Animal Speaking")*
> *#child class Dog inherits the base class Animal*
> *class Dog(Animal):*
> *def bark(self):*
> *print("barking dog")*
> *d = Dog()*
> *d.bark()*
> *d.speak()*

Output:

> *barking dog*
> *Animal Speaking*

Python Multi-Level inheritance

This inheritance has multiple levels in Python. Similarly, it has in other programming languages. This object-oriented feature is very useful to derive data from one class and to us it in another.

The syntax of multi-level inheritance:

Syntax:

class class1:
<class-suite>
class class2(class1):
<class suite>
class class3(class2):
<class suite>

Example:

class Animal:
def speak(self):
print("Speaking Animal")
#The child class Dog inherits the base class Animal
class Dog(Animal):
def bark(self):
print("barking dog")
#The child class Dogchild inherits another child class Dog
class DogChild(Dog):
def eat(self):
print("Bread eating...")
d = DogChild()
d.bark()
d.speak()
d.eat()

Output:

barking dog
Speaking Animal
Bread eating...

Python Multiple inheritance

Python gives the possibility to inherit multiple base classes in the child class.

Syntax

class Base1:
<class-suite>
class Base2:
<class-suite>
class BaseN:
<class-suite>

Example:

```
class Calculate1:
def Summation(self,a,b):
return a+b;
class Calculate2:
def Multiplication(self,a,b):
return a*b;
class Derive(Calculate1,Calculate2):
def Divide(self,a,b):
return a/b;
d = Derive()
print(isinstance(d,Derive))
```

Output:

True

Method Overriding

We can give specific implementation of the parent class method in our child class. Using or defining parent class method on a child class is called method over-riding.

Example:

```
class Bank:
def getroi(self):
return 10;
class SBI(Bank):
def getroi(self):
return 7;
class ICICI(Bank):
def getroi(self):
return 8;
a1 = Bank()
a2 = SBI()
a3 = ICICI()
print("Bank interest:",a1.getroi());
print("SBI interest:",a2.getroi());
print("ICICI interest:",a3.getroi());
```

Output:

```
Bank interest: 10
SBI interest: 7
ICICI interest: 8
```

Data abstraction in Python

Abstraction is a significant part of object-oriented programming. In Python, we can likewise perform data hiding by adding the twofold underscore (__) as a prefix to the credit that is to be covered up. After this, the property won't be noticeable outside of the class through the object.

Example:

```
class Employee:
count = 0;
def __init__(self):
Employee.__count = Employee.__count+1
def display(self):
print("The number of employees",Employee.__count)
emp = Employee()
emp2 = Employee()
try:
print(emp.__count)
finally:
1emp.display()
```

Output:

```
The number of employees 2
AttributeError: 'Employee' object has no attribute '__count'
```

Python magic method

Python magic method is defined as the uncommon method that includes "magic" to a class. It starts and finishes with twofold underscores, for instance, _init_ or _str_.

The built-in classes define numerous magic methods. The dir() capacity can be utilized to see the quantity of magic methods inherited by a class. It has two prefixes, and addition underscores in the method name.

It is mostly used to define the over-burden practices of predefined administrators.

__init__

The _init_ method is called after the making of the class; however, before it came back to the guest. It is invoked with no call, when an instance of the class is made like constructors in other programming dialects. For example, C++, Java, C#, PHP, and so forth. These methods are otherwise called initialize and are called after _new_. Its where you ought to initialize the instance factors.

__str__

This capacity processes "informal" or a pleasantly printable string portrayal of an object and should restore a string object.

__repr__

This capacity is called by the repr() built-in capacity to figure the "official" string portrayal of an object and returns a machine-discernible portrayal of a kind. The objective of the _repr_ is to be unambiguous.

__len__

This capacity should restore the object's length.

__call__

An object is made callable by adding the _call_ magic method, and it is another method that isn't required as frequently is _call_.

Whenever defined in a class, at that point that class can be called. In any case, in the event that it was a capacity instance itself instead of modifying.

__del__

Similarly, _init_ is a constructor method, _del_ and resembles a destructor. In the event that you have opened a document in _init _, at that point _del_ can close it.

__bytes__

It offers to figure a byte-string portrayal of an object and should restore a string object.

__ge__

This method gets invoked when >= administrator is utilized and returns True or False.

__neg__

This capacity gets required the unary administrator.

__ipow__

This capacity gets approached the types with arguments. For example, a**=b.

__le__

This capacity gets approached correlation using <= administrator.

nonzero

5.5 Python Stack and Queue

Python stacks and queue are the most basic functions. They are used to access the data to and to alter it for some purpose. These data structures are famous in computer software world. Queues have a rule FIFO (First In First Out) for sorting data, while stack follows LIFO (Last In First Out) method.

Stack Attributes:

push - It adds a component to the highest point of the stack.

pop - It expels a component from the highest point of the stack.

Tasks on Stack:

Addition – It increases the size of stack.

Cancellation – It is used to decrease the size of stack.

Traversing - It involves visiting every component of the stack.

Qualities:

- Insertion request of the stack is saved.

- Helpful for parsing the activities.

- Duplicacy is permitted.

Code

```
# Code to demonstrate Implementation of
# stack using list
y= ["Python-language", "Csharp", "Androidnew"]
y.push("Javaflash")
y.push("C++lang")
print(y)
print(y.pop())
print(y)
print(y.pop())
print(y)
```

Output:

```
['Python-language', 'Csharp', 'Androidnew', 'Javaflash', 'C++lang']
C++lang
['Python-language', 'Csharp', 'Androidnew', 'Javaflash']
Javaflash
['Python-language', 'Csharp', 'Androidnew']
```

Queue Attributes

First-in-First-Out (FIFO) principle allows queue to have elements from both ends. It is open to get in and let go of components.

Basic functionalities in queue:

enqueue – For adding elements.

dequeue – For removing elements from queue.

Qualities

- Insertion request of the queue is protected.

- Duplicacy is permitted.

- Valuable for parsing CPU task activities.

Code

```
import queue
# Queue is created as an object 'L'
L = queue.Queue(maxsize=10)
# Data is inserted in 'L' at the end using put()
L.put(9)
L.put(6)
L.put(7)
L.put(4)
# get() takes data from
# from the head
# of the Queue
print(L.get())
print(L.get())
print(L.get())
print(L.get())
```

Output:

9

6

7

4

Command line arguments in Python

Python focuses to provide command lines for input parameters that are passed to elements in order to execute functions.

By using getopt module, this operation is executed.

The getopt module of Python

It is very similar to other programming languages. It is used to pass inputs through command lines to get options from the user. It allows a user to input options.

Python Assert Keyword

These keywords inform the programmer about the realities of running the program. It works with conditional commands. When the condition doesn't get fulfilled, it declines with the display of an assertive message on the screen e.g. "no data is available". AssertionErrors are used to define the program properly.

Why Assertion?

It is a highly recommended debugging tool. It keeps the user aware about codes on each step. If some lines of codes have errors or mistakes, it alerts the user with message.

Syntax

assert condition, error_message(optional)

Example:

def avg(scores):
assert len(scores) != 0,"The List is empty."
return sum(scores)/len(scores)
scoresb = [67,59,86,75,92]
print("The Average of scoresb:",avg(scoresb))
scores1 = []
print("The Average of scoresa:",avg(scoresa))

Output:

The Average of scores2: 75.8
AssertionError: The List is empty.

Chapter 6

Python Basics

Python modules, exceptions and arrays are an integral part of object-oriented Python programming language. In data science, we use them from time to time to have a better understanding with the usage of code in a logical way. These programming methods are also used in other programming languages, and are a popular framework because of their usage to transform the complexities of programming into simple coding. Let's discuss them one by one.

6.1 Python Modules

Python modules are programs that have programming codes in Python. They contain all variables, classes and functions of this unique language. They enable the programmer to organize codes in a proper format that is logically valid. They can be imported to use the functionality of one module for another.

Example:

Now here a module named as file.py will be generated which contains a function func that has a code to print some message on the console.

So let's generate it **file.py.**

#displayMsg prints a message to the name.
def displayMsg(name)
print("Hi "+name);

Now it is required to add this module into the main module to call the method displayMsg() defined in the module named file.

Loading the module in our Python code
In order to utilize the functionality of Python code, the module is loaded. Python provides two types of statements as defined below.

1. The import statement

2. The from-import statement

Python Standard Library- Built-in Modules
There is an unlimited pool of Python Built-in Modules. We will discuss some of the most important modules. These are:

- **random**
- **statistics**
- **math**
- **datetime**
- **csv**

To import any of them, use this syntax:

Import[module_name]
eg. Import random

Random module in Python

This module is used to generate numbers. By using the command random(), we can generate float numbers. The range of these float numbers lies between 0.0 and 1.0.

Here are some important random functions used in random module:

The Function random.randint()
It is for random integers.

The Function random.randrange()
It is for randomly selected elements.

The Function random.choice()
It is for randomly selected elements from non-empty.

The Statistics module of Python
It is a very useful module of Python. It provides numerical data after performing statistics functions.

Here is a list of some very commonly used functions of this module:

The mean() function
It performs arithmetic mean of the list.

For Example:

import statistics
datalist = [5, 2, 7, 4, 2, 6, 8]
a= statistics.mean(datalist)
print("The Mean will be:", a)

The Mean will be: 4.857142857142857

The median() function

It gives middle value of the list.

Example:

import statistics
dataset = [4, -5, 6, 6, 9, 4, 5, -2]
print("Median of data-set is : % s "
% (statistics.median(dataset)))

Output:

Median of data-set is: 4.5

The mode() function

It provides common data from the list.

Example:

import statistics
datasets =[2, 4, 7, 7, 2, 2, 3, 6, 6, 8]
print("Calculated Mode % s" % (statistics.mode(datasets)))

Output:

Calculated Mode 2

The stdev() function

It calculates the standard deviation.

Example:

import statistics
sample = [7, 8, 9, 10, 11]
print("Standard Deviations of sample data is % s "
  % (statistics.stdev(sample)))

Output:

Standard Deviation of sample data is 1.5811388300841898

The median_low()

The median_low function is used to return the low median of numeric data in the list.

Example:

import statistics
 # simple list of a set of integers
set1 = [4, 6, 2, 5, 7, 7]
 # Print low median of the data-set
print ("data-set Low median is % s "
% (statistics.median_low(set1)))

Output:

Low median of the data-set is 5

median_high()

The median_high () function is employed to calculate the high median of numeric data in the list.

Example:

import statistics
 # list of set of the integers
dataset = [2, 1, 7, 6, 1, 9]
print("High median of data-set is %s "
* % (statistics.median_high(dataset)))*

Output:

High median of the data-set is 6

The math module of Python

This module contains the mathematical functions to perform every mathematical calculation.

Here are two constants as well:

Pie (n): A well-known mathematical constant and is defined as the ratio of circumstance to the diameter of a circle. Its value is 3.141592653589793.

Euler's number (e): It is the base of the natural logarithmic, and its value is 2.718281828459045.

A few math modules which are given below:

The math.log10() function

It calculates base1 0 logarithm of the number.

Example:

import math
x=13 # small value of of x
print('log10(x) is :', math.log10(x))

Output:

log10(x) is : 1.1139433523068367

The math.sqrt() function

It calculates the root of the number.

Example:

import math
x = 20
y = 14
z = 17.8995
print('sqrt of 20 is ', math.sqrt(x))
print('sqrt of 14 is ', math.sqrt(y))
print('sqrt of 17.8995 is ', math.sqrt(z))

Output:

sqrt of 20 is 4.47213595499958
sqrt of 14 is 3.7416573867739413
sqrt of 17.8995 is 4.230780069916185

The math.expm1() function

This method calculates e raised to the power of any number minus 1. e is the base of natural logarithm.

The math.cos() function

It calculates cosine of any number in radians.

Example:

```
import math
angleInDegree = 60
angleInRadian = math.radians(angleInDegree)
print('Given angle :', angleInRadian)
print('cos(x) is :', math.cos(angleInRadian))
```

Output:

```
Given angle : 1.0471975511965976
cos(x) is : 0.5000000000000001
```

The math.sin() function

It calculates the sine of any number, in radians.

Example:

```
import math
angleInDegree = 60
angleInRadian = math.radians(angleInDegree)
print('Given angle :', angleInRadian)
print('sin(x) is :', math.sin(angleInRadian))
```

Given angle: 1.0471975511965976
sin(x) is: 0.8660254037844386

The math.tan() function

It returns the tangent of any number, in radians.

Example:

import math
angleInDegree = 60
angleInRadian = math.radians(angleInDegree)
print('Given angle :', angleInRadian)
print('tan(x) is :', math.tan(angleInRadian))

Output:

Given angle : 1.0471975511965976
tan(x) is : 1.7320508075688767

The sys module of Python

This module provides access to system-specific functions. It changes the Python Runtime Environment to enable the user to get variables and parameters.

Need to import sys function

First, there is a need to import the sys module in the program before starting the use of functions.

The sys.modules' function

These functions perform some really important tasks on system in Python programming.

- **Function of sys.argv:** For arguments
- **Function of sys.base_prefix:** For startup
- **Function of sys.byteorder**: To get byterorder.
- **Function of sys.maxsize**: To get large integer.
- **Function of sys.path**: To set path.
- **Function of sys.stdin**: To restore files.
- **Function of sys.getrefcount**: To get reference count of an object.
- **Fun tion of sys.exit**: To exit from Python command prompt.
- **Function of sys executable**: Locate the Python in system.
- **sys.platform:** To identify Platform.

The Collection Module of Python

This module plays an important role, as it collects major data formats or data structures, such as list, dictionary, set, and tuple. It improves the functionality of the current version of Python. It is defined as a container that is employed to conserve collections of data, for example, list.

The function of namedtuple() in Collection Module

It produces a tuple object without causing an issue with indexing.

Examples:

```
John = ('John', 25, 'Male')
print(John)
```

('John', 25, 'Male')

OrderedDict() function

It generates dictionary object with key that can overwrite data inside.

Example:

import collections
d1=collections.OrderedDict()
d1['A']=15
d1['C']=20
d1['B']=25
d1['D']=30
for k,v in d1.items():
print (k,v)

Output:

A 15
C 20
B 25
D 30

Functin defaultdict()

It produces an object similar to dictionary.

Example:

from collections import defaultdict
number = defaultdict(int)

```
number['one'] = 1
number['two'] = 2
print(number['three'])
```

Output:

```
0
```

Counter() function

It counts the hasbale objects after reviewing the elements of list.

Example:

```
A = Counter()
Xlist = [1,2,3,4,5,7,8,5,9,6,10]
Counter(Xlist)
Counter({1:5,2:4})
Ylist = [1,2,4,7,5,1,6,7,6,9,1]
c = Counter(Ylist)
print(A[1])
```

Result:

```
3
```

The function deque()

It facilitates addition and removal of elements from both ends.

For Example:

```
from collections import deque
list = ["x","y","z"]
```

deq = deque(list)
print(deq)

Output:

deque(['x', 'y', 'z'])

Python OS Module

Python OS module provides functions utilized for interacting with the operating system and also obtains related data about it. The OS comes under Python's standard utility modulesPython OS module which allows you to work with the files, documents and directories. Some of OS module functions are as follows:

os.name

It provides the name of the operating system module it imports.

It can register 'posix', 'nt', 'os2', 'ce', 'java' and 'riscos'.

Example:

import os
print(os.name)

Output:

posix

os.getcwd()

It restores the Current Working Directory (CWD) of the file.

Example:

> *import os*
> *print(os.getcwd())*

Output:

> *C:\Users\Python\Desktop\ModuleOS*

os.error

The functions in this module define the OS level errors in case of invalid file names and path.

Example:

> *import os*
> *filename1 = 'PythonData.txt'*
> *f = open(filename1, 'rU')*
> *text = f.read()*
> *f.close()*
> *print('Difficult read: ' + filename1)*

Output:

> *Difficult read: PythonData.txt*

os.popen()

It opens a file, and it gives back a fileobject that contains connection with pipe.

The datetime Module

It is an imported module that allows you to create date and time objects. It works to conduct many functions related to date and time.

Let's understand it through an example:

Example:

> *import datetime;*
> *#returns the current datetime object*
> *print(datetime.datetime.now())*

Output:

> *2018-12-18 16:16:45.462778*

Python read csv file

The Comma Separated values (CSV) File

It is a simple file format that arranges tabular data. It is used to store data in tabular form ora spreadsheet that can be exchanged when needed. It is in a Microsoft excel supported data form.

The CSV Module Functions in Python

This module helps in reading/writing CSV files. It takes the data from columns and stores it to use in the future.

- **The function csv.field_size_limit -** To maximize field size.

- **The function csv.reader –** To read information or data from a csv file.

- **The function csv.writer** – To write the information or data to a csv file

These functions have a major role in CSV module.

6.2 The Exceptions in Python

Exceptions are actually interruptions that stops the running program. They are mistakes or errors in the code. In Python, these are handled differently.

The Common Exceptions in Python

Here are some common exceptions that may occur in Python. Every Python programmer is very familiar with these errors or exceptions.

- **The exception of ZeroDivisionError:** when a number is divided by zero.

- **The exception of NameError:** when a name is not found.

- **The exception of IndentationError:** when incorrect indentation is given.

- **The exception of IOError:** when Input Output operation fails.

- **The exception of EOFError:** when the end of the file is reached, and still operations are being performed.

Unhandled Exceptions

Example:

```
x= int(input("Enter a:"))
y = int(input("Enter b:"))
z= a/b;
```

```
print("x/y = %d"%c)
print("Hello I am a teacher")
```

Output:

```
Enter a:10
Enter b:0
Traceback (most recent call last):
File "exception-test.py", line 3, in <module>
  c = a/b;
ZeroDivisionError: division by zero
```

The finally block

It is used to run a code before the try statement.

Syntax

```
try:
# block of code
# this may throw an exception
finally:
# block of code
# this will always be executed
```

Example:

```
try:
fileptr = open("file.txt","r")
try:
fileptr.write("Hi I am good")
finally:
fileptr.close()
print("file closed")
```

```
except:
    print("Error")
```

Output:

file closed
Error

The Exception Raising in Python

The raise clause in Python is used to raise an exception.

Syntax

Raise exception_class,<value>

The Custom Exception in Python

It enables programmers to generate exceptions that have already been launched with the program.

Example:

```
class ErrorInCode(Exception):
def __init__(self, data):
self.data = data
def __str__(self):
return repr(self.data)
try:
raise ErrorInCode(2000)
except ErrorInCode as ae:
print("Received error:", ae.data)
```

Received error: 2000

6.3 Python Arrays

Array is a set of elements that are used to work on specific data values. It is advanced level programming that allows users multiple functionality over data structures. Through arrays, code can be simplified, therefore saving a lot of time.

Array Element - Data element stored in array.

Array Index - Position of an element.

Array Representation:
The declaration of array can be done in many different ways.

- Array Index starts with 0.

- Element can be located with the help of its index number.

- The length of the array defines the storage capacity of the elements.

Array operations in Python:
Some of the basic operations in an array are given below:

- **Traverse** – To print all the elements one by one.

- **Insertion** – Addition of element in Index.

- **Deletion** – Deletion of element at index.

- **Search** – To search the element.

- **Update** - To update an element at the given index.

Array Generation

*array **import** ***

MyarrayName = array(typecode, [initializers])

Accessing array elements

The array elements accessibility can be ensured by using the respective indices of those elements.

import array as arr
a = arr.array('i', [1, 3, 5, 87])
print("First element:", a[0])
print("Second element:", a[1])
print("Second last element:", a[-1])

Output:

First element: 1
Second element: 3
Second last element: 8

Arrays are changeable, and elements can be changed in similar to lists.

A combination of arrays makes the process speedy and saves time. The array can reduce the code's size.

Deletion can be done by using the **del** statement in Python.

The length of an array can be described as the number of elements in an array. It returns an integer value that is equal to the total number of the elements present in that array.

Syntax

len(array_name)

Example:

a=arr.array('d',[1.2 , 2.2 ,3.2,3,6,7.8])
b=arr.array('d',[4.5,8.6])
c=arr.array('d')
c=a+b
print("Array c = ",c)

Output:

Array c= array('d', [1.2, 2.2, 3.2, 3.6, 7.8, 4.5, 8.6])

Example:

import *array as arr*
x = arr.array('i', [5, 10, 15, 20])
print("First element:", x[0])
print("Second element:", x[1])
print("Second last element:", x[-1])

Output:

First element: 5
Second element: 10
Second last element: 15

Chapter 7

Python Data Science Libraries and General Libraries

In the previous chapters, we discussed the important concepts of Python, such as data structures, built-in functions, variable, exceptions, methods, for loops and if statements. Now, we will study the modules and packages of Python that is important for any project.

Python programming and data science are integral to one another. Python is an unbelievable language for data science and the individuals who need to begin in the field of data science. It bolsters countless cluster libraries and systems to give a decision for working with data science in a spotless and productive manner. The different systems and libraries accompany a particular reason for use, and should be picked by your prerequisite.

7.1 Python Data Science Libraries

A Python library is a gathering of capacities and techniques that aid in finishing explicit assignments. There are highly advanced libraries employed by developers for various tasks. In the beginning, Data Science and Python was considered unsuitable for each other, and now Python is very much connected with statistics, machine learning, and predictive analytics, as well as simple data analytics tasks. It is getting more accessible and useful day-by-day, as it is an open-source language. There are millions of data scientists who are enriching the language with tools through advanced coding. Now, there are highly advanced packages and libraries that data scientists are using for multiple data analysis tasks.

A brief description of some of the best Python libraries is given below

Numpy

NumPy is a very crucial Python library implied for logical registering. It accompanies support for an amazing N-dimensional exhibit item and broadcasting capacities.

Additionally, NumPy offers Fourier changes, arbitrary number capacities, and devices for coordinating C/C++ and Fortran code. Having a working understanding of NumPy is obligatory for full stack developers associated with AI ventures utilizing Python.

Numpy is the most fundamental, and a fantastic bundle, for working with information in Python. On the off chance that you are getting down to business on information investigation or Machine learning ventures, at that point, having a strong comprehension of numpy is required.

Different bundles for information investigation (like pandas) is based on numpy and the scikit-learn package that is utilized to assemble AI applications.

What does numpy provide?

At the center, numpy gives the phenomenal ndarray objects; short for n-dimensional clusters. In a 'ndarray' object, otherwise known as 'exhibit', you can store numerous things of similar information. It is the offices around the exhibit object that makes numpy advantageous for performing math and information controls.

Salient Features

· It is a very interactive library and it's easy to use.

· Mathematical problems are solved with ease.

Pandas

In Python, we use two-dimensional tables to analyze data, like in SQL or Excel. Initially, Python didn't have this feature. But that's why Pandas is so famous. Without a doubt, Pandas is the "*SQL of Python.*" In short, Pandas is the library that will help us to handle two-dimensional data tables in Python. In many ways, it's similar to SQL, though.

The Pandas' library is not exclusively a focal segment of the information science toolbox, yet it is utilized for different libraries in that accumulation.

Pandas is based on the NumPy bundle, which means a great deal of the structure of NumPy is utilized or duplicated in Pandas. Information in pandas is frequently used to bolster factual examination in SciPy, plotting capacities from Matplotlib, and machine learning calculations in Scikit-learn.

Jupyter Notebooks offer a decent situation for utilizing pandas to do information investigation and demonstrating, yet pandas can likewise be used in content tools.

Jupyter Notebooks enable us to execute code in a specific cell instead of running the whole record. This spares a lot of time when working with enormous datasets and complex changes. Scratchpad, likewise, gives a simple method to imagine pandas' DataFrames and plots.

Pandas is prominently known for giving information outlines in Python. This is a fantastic library for information examination, contrasted with other explicit dialects like R. By utilizing Pandas, it's simpler to deal with missing information, bolsters working with contrastingly filed information assembled from numerous various assets, and supports programmed information arrangement. It also provides devices information examination and information structures, like consolidating, molding or cutting datasets, and it is additionally exceptionally viable in working with information identified with time arrangement. The function works by giving hearty apparatuses to stacking information from Excel, level documents, databases, and a quick HDF5 group.

Utilizing the Pandas library makes it simpler and instinctive for developers to work with named or social data. It offers expressive, quick, and adaptable data structures. Pandas fills in as the essential elevated level structure for doing genuine data examination utilizing Python.

One of the most prominent and dominant features of Pandas is to interpret complex data activities utilizing negligible directions. Also, the AI library has no shortage of worked in techniques for consolidating, separating, and gathering data. It additionally

highlights time-arrangement usefulness.

Salient Features:

- Operations of custom type can be completed easily.

- Data manipulation becomes simpler and easier.

- When employed with other Python libraries and tools ,it gives excellent results.

The Matplotlib

Matplotlib is a two-dimensional plotting library with extraordinary representation modules for the Python programming language. It is equipped for delivering top-notch figures in various printed version organizations and intelligent cross-stage conditions. Besides being utilized in Python shell, Python contents, and IPython shell, Matplotlib can likewise be utilized in:

· Jupyter Notebook

· Web application servers

· GUI toolboxes; GTK+, Tkinter, Qt, and wxPython

As indicated by the official site of Matplotlib, the Python library attempts to "make simple things simple and hard things conceivable." The 2D plotting Python library permits producing bar graphs, mistake diagrams, histograms, plots, scatterplots, etc. with fewer lines of code.

Probably the best advantage is that it permits visual access to enormous measures of information in effectively absorbable visuals. Matplotlib comprises of a few plots, like line, bar, disperse, and histograms.

Matplotlib represents a Mathematical Plotting Library in Python. It is a library that is for the most part utilized for information representation, including 3D plots, histograms, picture plots, scatterplots, bar graphs, and power spectra. It includes bright highlights for zooming and searching for gold in various printed copy designs. It bolsters practically all systems, for example, Windows, Mac, and Linux. This library also fills in as an augmentation for the NumPy library. Matplotlib has a module pyplot that is utilized in representations, which is frequently contrasted with MATLAB.

These libraries are the best for amateurs to begin information science utilizing the Python programming language. There are numerous other Python libraries accessible. For example, NLTK for standard language preparing, Pattern for web mining, Theano for profound learning. IPython and Scrapy for web scratching. Also, Mlpy and Statsmodels; the sky is the limit from there. Be that as it may, for novices beginning wihh information science in Python, it is an absolute necessity to be knowledgeable about the top libraries.

Salient Features

- It has handy properties, font properties, line styles, etc. through an object-oriented interface.

- Scatter's Legend

- MATLAB interface for simple plotting of data.

- It has secondary x/y axis support to represent 2-dimmensions.

- It is supports many operating systems.

Scikit-Learn

Scikit-learn gives a scope of administered and solo learning calculations by means of a predictable interface in Python. It is authorized under a lenient rearranged BSD permit and is dispersed under numerous Linux disseminations, empowering scholastic and business use. The library is based upon the SciPy (Scientific Python) that must be introduced before you can utilize scikit-learn.

There are a few Python libraries that give a strong execution to the scope of machine learning calculations. Outstanding amongst others is Scikit-Learn, a bundle that gives proficient adaptations of countless basic calculations. Scikit-Learn is described as a perfect, uniform, and streamlined API, is extremely helpful and has complete online documentation. One advantage is the consistency. Once you comprehend the fundamental use and language structure of Scikit-Learn for one model, changing to another model or calculation is very direct.

Undoubtedly, the fanciest things in Python are Machine Learning and Prescient Investigation. Also, the best library for that is Scikit-Learn, which essentially characterizes itself as "Machine Learning in Python." Scikit-Learn has a few techniques, fundamentally covering all that you may require in the initial couple of long periods of your information profession: relapse strategies, characterization strategies, and bunching, model approval and model determination.

This prevalent library is utilized for AI in information science with different order, relapse and grouping calculations. It offers help with vector machines, innocent Bayes, angle boosting, and sensible relapse. SciKit is intended to interoperate with SciPy and NumPy.

Salient Features

- Capability to extract features from images and text

- Can be utilized again in several contexts

Scipy

There is scipy library and scipy stack. The vast majority of the libraries and bundles are a piece of the Scipy stack (for logical processing in Python). One of these parts is the Scipy library, which gives proficient answers for numerical schedules (the math stuff behind AI models). These include incorporation, introduction, improvement, and so forth. Scipy gives scientific strategies to do the unpredictable AI forms in Scikit-learn.

It is an open-source library utilized for registering different modules, for example, picture preparing, joining, insertion, unique capacities, enhancements, straight variable based math, Fourier Transform, grouping, and numerous different undertakings. This library is utilized with NumPy to perform proficient numerical calculations.

Salient Features

- Comfortably handles mathematical operations.

- Provides effective and efficient numerical routines, such as numerical integration and optimization, using sub-modules.

- Supports signal processing.

TensorFlow

Anyone engaged with AI machine learning tasks utilizing Python must have knowledge of TensorFlow. Created by Google, it is an open-source representative math library for numerical calculations utilizing information stream diagrams. The scientific activities in a normal TensorFlow information stream diagram are spoken to by the chart hubs. The chart edges speak to the multidimensional information exhibits, a.k.a. tensors, that stream between the diagram hubs.

TensorFlow parades an adaptable design. It enables Python engineers to convey calculations to one or numerous CPUs or GPUs in a work area, cell phone, or server, without the need for revising code. All libraries made in TensorFlow are written in C and C++. Broadly utilized Google items, like Google Photos and Google Voice Search, are constructed utilizing TensorFlow. The library has a convoluted front-end for Python. The Python code will get accumulated and after that executed on TensorFlow.

Salient Features

- Allows preparing various neural systems and numerous GPUs, making models exceptionally productive for enormous scale frameworks.

- Easily trainable on CPU and GPU for disseminated figuring.

- Flexibility in its operability, which means TensorFlow offers the choice of taking out the parts that you need and leaving what you don't.

- Great level of network and designer support.

- Unlike other information science Python libraries, TensorFlow improves the way toward imagining every single piece of the diagram.

Keras

It is recognized as one of the coolest AI (Algorithm) Python libraries. Keras offers a simpler instrument for communicating neural systems. It also features extraordinary utilities for accumulating models, preparing datasets, imagining charts, and significantly more. Written in Python, Keras can keep running over CNTK, TensorFlow, and Theano. The Python AI library is created with an essential spotlight on permitting quick experimentation. All Keras models are compact.

Contrasted with other Python AI libraries, Keras is moderate. This is because of the way that it makes a computational diagram utilizing the backend framework first, and after that uses the equivalent to perform activities. Keras is extremely expressive and adaptable for doing creative research.

Salient Features

- Being totally Python-based makes it simple to troubleshoot and investigate.

- Modular in nature.

- Neural system models can be joined for growing increasingly complex models.

- Runs easily on both CPU and GPU.

- Supports practically all models of a neural system, including convolutional, inserting, completely associated, pooling, and repetitive.

Seaborn

Fundamentally an information perception library for Python, Seaborn is based over the Matplotlib library. Additionally, it is firmly incorporated with Pandas information structures. The Python information perception library offers an abnormal state interface for drawing appealing factual charts.

The primary point of Seaborn is to make representation an imperative piece of investigating and getting information. Its dataset-arranged plotting capacities work on exhibits and information edges containing entire datasets. The library is perfect for inspecting connections among numerous factors. Seaborn makes all the significant semantic mapping and measurable collections for creating educational plots. The Python information representation library also has devices for picking shading palettes that guide you in uncovering designs in a dataset.

Salient Features

- Automatic estimation; the plotting of direct relapse models.

- Comfortable perspectives on the general structure of complex datasets.

- Eases building complex representations, utilizing abnormal state deliberations for organizing multi-plot matrices.

- Options for picturing bivariate or univariate disseminations.

- Specialized support for utilizing clear cut factors.

Natural Language Toolkit (NLTK)

Valuable for common language preparing and design acknowledgment undertakings. It can be utilized to create intellectual models, tokenization, labeling, thinking and different assignments helpful to AI applications

Salient Features

- Comes with a linguistic structure tagger.

- Supports lexical assessment.

7.2 Python General Libraries

Python is named as a "batteries-included programming language." This essentially implies it accompanies various pre-packaged libraries. In any case, there are an abundance of different libraries accessible for the translated, abnormal state, universally useful programming language.

Among different elements adding to the prevalence of Python, having a humongous gathering of libraries is a noteworthy one. The more libraries and bundles a programming language has available to it, the more assorted use-cases it can have.

Requests

One of the most prominent general Python libraries is Requests that make HTTP demand less difficult and increasingly human-accommodating. Authorized under the Apache2 permit and written in

Python, Requests is the true standard utilized by engineers for making HTTP demands in Python.

Notwithstanding utilizing the Requests library for sending HTTP solicitations to a server, it also permits including structure information, content, header, multi-part documents, and so forth with them. With the library, designers need not to add a question to the URL or structure encode the POST information physically.

The Requests library abstracts the various complexities of making HTTP demands in a basic API so designers can concentrate more on communicating with administrations. The library offers authority support for Python 2.7, 3.4 or more and works incredibly well on PyPy, as well.

Salient Features:

- Allows multipart record transfers and spilling downloads.

- Automatic substance disentangling and programmed decompression.

- Browser-style SSL confirmation.

- Features can be modified and improved according to prerequisites.

- Keep-Alive and Connection Pooling Supports international domains and URLs.

Pillow

Python Imaging Library or PIL is a free Python library that adds a picture preparing capacity to the Python interpreter. In basic terms, PIL permits controlling and opening, and different picture records organized in Python. Made by Alex Clark and Contributors, Pillow is a fork of the PIL library.

Notwithstanding offering incredible picture handling abilities, Pillow offers powerful inward portrayal and broad record organization support. The center Python library is intended to offer quick access to information.

Salient Features:

- Effective investigating bolster utilizing the show() strategy.

- Ideal for group handling applications.

- Identifies and peruses a huge scope of picture document designs.

- Offers BitmapImage, PhotoImage, and Window DIB interfaces.

- Supports discretionary relative changes, shading space transformations, separating with a lot of implicit convolution parts, picture resizing and turning, and point activities.

- The histogram technique permits hauling a few measurements out of a picture, and can be utilized for programmed upgrade and worldwide factual investigation.

Scrapy

Scrapy is a free and open-source Python structure that is broadly utilized for web scratching and various different assignments, including mechanized testing and information mining. At first, Scrapy was created for web scratching but has advanced to satisfy different purposes. The library offers a quick and abnormal state strategy for creeping sites and separating organized information from website pages.

Written in Python, Scrapy is works around bugs that are essentially independent crawlers, which are given a lot of guidelines. Complying with the DRY standard, Scrapy makes it simpler to assemble and scale undeniable web slithering undertakings.

Salient Features:

- Easy to compose a bug to slither a site and concentrate information.

- Follows the DRY rule.

- Offers a web-slithering shell that enables engineers to test a site's conduct.

- Supports sending out scratched information utilizing the direction line.

Tkinte

When utilized with Tkinter, Python offers a simple and quick path for making GUI applications. It is considered the standard GUI library for the Python programming language. It offers an amazing item situated interface for the Tk GUI toolbox. Making a GUI application utilizing Tkinter is simple. You can simply pursue these basic advances:

- Import Tkinter

- Create the primary window for the GUI application; a work in progress

- Add at least one Tkinter Widget

- Enter the headliner circle for making a move for every client activated occasion.

Tkinter is Graphical User Interface (GUI) library that has powerful modules to create a user interface.

Salient Features:

- Comes with a scope of gadgets that help geometry the executive's strategies.

- Eases creating GUI applications.

- Supports a powerful object-situated interface.

Six

Owing to the fact that it's the simplest Python library, Six is an amazing Python library that is intended to smooth out the contrasts between different Python 2 and Python 3. Six is used for supporting codebases that can work on both Python 2 and Python 3 without the need for adjustments.

The Six libraries is super-simple to utilize on account of it being offered as a solitary Python document. Consequently, it is absurdly simple to duplicate the library into a Python venture. The name Six reflects (Python) 2 x (Python) 3.

Salient Features:

- Simple utility capacities for making Python code perfect with Python 2 and Python 3.

- Supports each adaptation since Python 2.6.

- Easy to use because its contained in a solitary Python document.

Pygame

Pygame is a free and open-source Python library that is intended for achieving sight and sound application improvements in Python, particularly two-dimensional gaming ventures. Thus, it is generally utilized by both beginner and expert Python game engineers. Pygame utilizes the SDL (Simple DirectMedia Layer) library. Like the SDL library, Pygame library is profoundly convenient and subsequently offers help for a wide number of stages and working frameworks.

It is conceivable to port applications created utilizing Pygame on Android-fueled gadgets, as well as cell phones and tablets. For this very reason, pgs4a (Pygame subset for Android) should be utilized.

Salient Features:

- Doesn't request OpenGL.

- Simple for utilizing multi-center CPUs.

- No GUI required for utilizing every single accessible capacity.

- Provides support for a wide scope of stages and working frameworks.

- Simple to utilize.

- Uses Assembly code and advanced C code for actualizing center capacities.

Bokeh

An instinctive portrayal library for the Python programming language, Bokeh grants imagining data in a stunning and critical course inside contemporary web programs. The data portrayal library encourages the creation of dashboards, data applications, and keen plots.

Despite offering brief and lovely improvement of versatile plans, the Bokeh library extends its capacity with tip top knowledge over spilling or tremendous datasets.

- Authentic plots with clear headings can be built easily without complexity.

- Bokeh portrayals can be successfully introduced into two of the most standard Python frameworks: Django and Flask.

- Capable of making dazzling and natural data recognitions Multiple language ties (Julia, Lua, Python, and R).

Asyncio

This library is used for composing simultaneous code utilizing the async/anticipates grammar by the developers. In larger part, the asyncio library is perfect for IO-bound and elevated level organized system code.

Asyncio has been utilized for different Python nonconcurrent frameworks that offer database association libraries, circulated undertaking lines, elite system and web servers, and significantly more. The library accompanies various elevated level and low-level APIs.

Salient Features

- Implementation of protocols by employing transport.

- Codes are simple and easy.

- Helps in generation of various loops.

7.3 Python Data Science Frameworks

Python frameworks provide a great utility to developers because they are considered a necessary time saving tools. They allow software engineers to deliver products quicker by providing a ready-made structure for application development, and by reducing the number of code.

Frameworks enable developers to be quick and responsive for the development of applications. They also allow the software engineers to reduce the number of codes employed.

Types of Python Frameworks

Full-Stack Framework

Full stack framework gives developers the utility of a one stop solution. These are as follows:

- Django

- Pyramid

- Turbo gears

- Web2py

- Cubicweb

- Giotto

- Pylon

Django

Django is one of the most exceptional and adaptable Python frameworks used. This full-stack, open-source framework focuses on decreasing the improvement of web application time. It achieves this through an open source system. The system is continually releasing new modules and code to unravel the methodology.

Django has multiple modules with an arrangement to access outside libraries' functions. It is very popular framework because of its large quantity of functions. Programmers prefer to use this framework in their programs as it is really supportive. They wish to promote it among the programmers specialists to improve its open-source libraries innovation and access.

Salient Features

- Large amount of readily available libraries.

- Web servers get support and assistance with it.

- Allows mandatory URL routing.

TurboGears

This framework is also open source and expects to make web application progression a much smoother and faster process.

The framework relies upon Ruby on the Rails and was built using the model-see controller plan. It empowers creators to re-reason business basics across stages and abatement the proportion of made code.

Creators would like to release a "negligible mode" later on, which will fill in as a smaller scale framework. This stripped-down variation will enable experts to build direct programming quickly, and save time and cash.

Salient Features:

- Function decorators: All features are implemented.

- Has command-line.

- Integration with MochiKit JavaScript library.

- Supports Multi-databases.

- Architecture MVC-style.

Pyramid

Pyramid is an ultra-versatile, lightweight Python framework. Developers as a rule use Pyramid to get basic web applications completely operational as quickly as possible.

The marketing behind Pyramid implies the framework is "the starting close to nothing, complete gigantic, stay finished framework." It functions as shown by the standard of control, which makes it a mind blowing elective for experienced specialists.

Salient Features:

- Versatility in authorization.
- Gives decorators for functions.
- Built in renderers available.

CubicWeb

Designed and generated by Logilab, CubicWeb is an allowed to-utilize, semantic, open-source, Python-based web system. In view of the information model, CubicWeb requires the equivalent characterized so as to build up a useful application.

Not at all like other famous Python structures that utilization separate perspectives and models; has CubicWeb utilized block. Various 3D shapes are then consolidated for making an occasion with the assistance of a database, a web server, and some design documents.

Salient features:

- Support OWL (Web Ontology Language) and RDF (Resource Description Framework).

- Components are reusable.

- Security work processes.

- Simplifies information related questions with RQL (Relational Query Language).

- Support for numerous databases.

Giotto

In light of the Model View Controller design, Giotto is an application system for Python. So as to permit website specialists, web engineers, and framework administrator's to work autonomously, Giotto isolates Model, View, and Controller components.

Giotto incorporates controller modules that empower clients to make applications over the web, IRC (Internet Relay Chat), and order line.

Salient Features:

- Automatic URL steering.

- Database steadiness with SQLAlchemy.

- Extremely concise code.

- Functional CRUD designs.

- Generic models and perspectives.

- Inbuilt reserve with help for Memcache and Redis (Available API for expanding support for different motors).

- Jinja2 for HTML layouts (API accessible for supporting other format motors).

Arch

Pythons Framework is an open-source Python-put together structure that concentrations with respect to the quick improvement of utilizations. The structure is planned by joining probably the best components and properties of dialects including Perl, Python, and Ruby.

It is accessible although in support mode. A few designers still utilize the Pylons system because of its capacity to offer an exceptionally adaptable structure for web improvement. To advance reusability, the full-stack structure utilizes WSGI (Web Server Gateway Interface).

Salient features:

- HTML form validation and generation.

- Routes.

- Text-based templating.

- URL dispatch.

- URL mapping dependent on Routes setup by means of WebHelpers.

Micro frameworks

Miniaturized scale frameworks don't give extra functionalities and highlights. For example, database deliberation layer, structure approval, and explicit apparatuses and libraries. Developers utilizing a miniaturized scale framework includes many codes, and extra necessities, such as:

- Flask
- Bottle
- Cherrypy
- Dash
- Falcon
- Hug
- Morepath
- Pycnic

Flask

It allows the developers to make a secure web application establishment from where it turns into a potential to utilize any expansions required. The miniaturized scale framework is perfect with Google App Engine. Tried by the Sinatra Ruby framework, the miniaturized scale framework requires Jinja2 layout and Werkzeug WSGI toolbox. Flask is versatile for clients given its lightweight and measured structure.

Notable Features:

- Built-in quick debugger.

- Inbuilt advancement server.

- Jinja2 templating.

- Support for connecting any ORM.

Bottle

Bottle creates a source record for each application utilizing it. Aside from the Python Standard Library, Bottle doesn't demonstrate conditions required for making little web applications.

Out of the numerous preferences of utilizing Bottle, the real one is that it enables developers to work near the equipment. Notwithstanding building short-sighted individual use applications, Bottle is an adept fit for learning the association of web frameworks and prototyping.

- Adapter support for outsider format motors and WSGI/HTTP servers

- Plugin support for various databases

- Gives demand dispatching courses having URL-parameter support

CherryPy

CherryPy is a remarkable open-source, object-oriented Python framework. Any CherryPy-controlled web application is a free Python application with its very own embedded multi-hung web server and continues running on any OS with assistance for Python.

There is no prerequisite for an Apache server for running applications made using CherryPy. The little scale framework allows the developer(s) to use any advancement for data and templating.

Salient features

- A number of out-of-the-case instruments for affirmation, saving, encoding, sessions, static substance, and significantly more

- A versatile understood module framework

- Consideration, profiling, and testing is done with the help of in-built support.

- Offers straightforwardness for running different HTTP servers simultaneously

- It has a robust structure framework

Dash

Run is an open-source Python-based structure for structure insightful applications based on the web. This framework is ideal for data analysts that aren't into the mechanics of web improvement.

Salient Features:

- No standard code for starting

- Customization is of high level

- It contains support of plugins.

- it hase a simple interface for tying UI controls, including dropdowns, outlines, and sliders

- URL coordinating (Dash Deployment Server)

Falcon

Falcon is a widely used Python structure across the world. It is micro-framework that enables HTTP and REST models for licensed Python programmers.

As indicated by the benchmark test-driven by Sanic, Falcon can manage more requests than all other micro-frameworks. The Python framework intends to have 100% code incorporation. Bird of prey is used by tremendous players like LinkedIn, OpenStack, and RackSpace.

Salient Features:

- An extensible, incredibly streamlined code base.

- DRY requesting planning through middleware sections and catches.

- Extra speed help with Cython support.

- Unit testing by means of WSGI assistants and ridicules

Hug

The Hug is intended to enable Python engineers to build up an API. The Python structure streamlines API improvement through multiple methods for offering various interfaces. It is marked as the quickest web structure for Python 3.

Whether you are doing neighborhood advancement or over HTTP or using the CLI, Hug gives you a chance to finish application improvements rapidly and effectively. To take execution to the next level, Hug devours assets just when required and uses Cython for arrangement.

MorePath

It is marked as the "Too Powered Python Web Framework,". MorePath guarantees insignificant arrangement impression. It is planned explicitly for getting the vast majority of the run of the mill go through cases and running ASAP, including the regular Python data structures being initiated into RESTful Web Services.

The micro framework, MorePath, is a genuinely adaptable model-driven web system.

Salient features:

- All perspectives are conventional.

- Comes with all the essential apparatuses to create restful web administrations

- Creating conventional UIs is as basic as subclassing

- Extensible with a straightforward, lucid, and general expansion and abrogate instrument

- Flexible, straightforward, and amazing authorizations

Pycnic

Pycnic is an object orriented micro framework accepted to be the quickest for structure JSON-based APIs. The little, independent, and streamlined for JSON-based APIs system can hold its ground well among enormous players. Since Pycnic makes only the Web APIs, it has a negligible impression and in this manner, it is quick.

Salient features:

- Built-in blunder dealing with

- Capable of taking care of JSON-based solicitations

- Handles routing

Asynchronous Framework

An asynchronous framework is a microframework that permits for handling a broad set of concurrent connections. Usually, an asynchronous framework made for Python utilizes the programming language's asyncio library.

- Sanic

- Tornado

- Growler

Tornado

The Tornado is an open-source Python system and a non-concurrent organizing library. It has multiple features that focus on authentication and authorization processes. While settling the C10k issue (which intends to deal with 10k associations at some random time), the unique structure utilizes a non-blocking system I/O.

The Python system was initially made for an organization called FriendFeed, which was procured by Facebook in 2009. The Tornado is considered as a perfect device for structure applications requesting superior and a few thousand simultaneous clients.

Salient Features

- Permits the implementation of 3rd-party authentication and authorization schemes
- Provides high-quality output
- Real-time services
- Supports translation and localization
- User authentication support
- It has Web Templating

Growler

Aspired by the NodeJS and the Express/Connect systems, Growler is a small-scale web structure composed on the Python's asyncio library. In contrast to other ordinary Python systems, demands in Growler aren't taken care of in the structure.

A top decision among Python systems for effectively and rapidly actualizing complex applications, Growler was initially created to figure out how to utilize asyncio library at its most reduced levels.

Salient Features

- Easy to use to montor the flow of program
- Supportive to open source packages
- Syntax of code is clean as it uses decorators

AIOHTTP

It is a dominant Python framework that has unique features: async and awaits. It uses asyncio library, that's why it is known as an asynchronous framework. It is both a server and client framework.

Salient Features

- Allows effectively building the views

- Middle-wares support

- Pluggable routing

- Best Signals

Chapter 8

Python Interpreters, Compilers, IDEs and Text Editor

Python interpreters, compilers, IDEs and Text Editor play a mandatory role in Python programming. It has multiple applications to execute major complex calculations in a very simplified method.

8.1 Python Interpreters

In Python, many interpreters work to align, manipulate and refine the programming codes. Python is employed and executed in different ways. Python programming is carried out with the help of a large quantity of interpreters. This high-level programming language is very easy to understand and execute.

It is depicted as a program that executes the guidelines written as codes. Execution is done directly so it can be said there is no need for the guidelines to be put into any programming software.

The following is a list of best interpreters used in Python programming language:

Interpreter- CPython:

It supports up to 3.7 Version of Python. CPython is the commonly available interpreter of Python language. It provides an outside capacity for many software.

CPython can be named a compiler.

It is very supportive to all platforms and provides a smooth experience to all users. This interpreter is famous because of the high demands of the software engineers, professionals, and computer language experts.

Interpreter- IronPython

IronPython is one of the most utilized interpreter of the Python language. It was generated by Jim Hugunin and was responsible for its upgrading to Version 1.0 that got released in 2006. After Version 1.0, it has been maintained by Microsoft. IronPython has numerous features, with the most prominent one is that it is completely written in C language. Most of the codes are automatically generated with the help of a code generator that is written in Python.

IronPython interpreter has affiliation with two libraries: Python and .NET framework. It possesses tools that directly attach it with visual studio. This feature of IronPython is quite a unique one, and due to this, it is highly demanded by program developers as it gives them the utility of visual studio as well. The console of Python is also very interactive. Moreover, it allows dynamic ways to interpret other languages

Interpreter- Jython

Jython is an interpreter that was formerly called JPython. Jython is implemented on the platform of Java. Jython was developed in late 1990's to change C with Java for enhanced performance. Jython contains excellent specifications and features. It has the function of dynamic and static compiling that allows software engineers to perform multiple tasks. Program in Jython utilizes Java scripts and modules rather than using the modules of Python.

Another salient feature of Jython is that it links the Python database with Java Virtual Machine.

Jython permits the users to import any Java class, like Python module. Developers can write codes first in Java and then transform it to Python. Due to this ability, it is considered as one of the top choices of developers throughout the world.

Interpreter-PyPy

Pypy is very quick and is used as an alternative for Python language. It was created in 2002. Its primary feature is that its closely related to CPython in context to execution and display. Python latest version is speedier than CPython. One primary reason for that is CPython acts only as an interpreter, and PyPy can also be utilized as a compiler. It is more flexible, versatile, and efficient than CPython, and supports many codes for Python language as well as other languages. Pypy also gives support to dynamic languages. That's why It is favorite to all programmers.

Interpreter- Stackless Python

Stackless Python is another efficient type of interpreter. It was released in 1998. It supports up to Python Version 3.7. It avoids using C stack. Stackless Python has a predominant feature of micro-threads. The feature allows avoiding the burden of the overhead associated with the standard operating system threads. Stackless Python assists with communication channels and routine tasks scheduling. Stackless Python is used in the programming of games. Various Python libraries also utilize it. Most of the Stackless Python features have resemblance with Pypy, as well.

8.2 Compilers in Python

A compiler is a code translator software that transforms the code from one programming language to another. There are many compilers in Python that have a specified language conversion system. They are used to make the program executable through formatting, aligning, and correction of code.

CPython compiler is one of the best compilers that is acknowledged by programmers and officials in IT industry.

Some other good Python Compilers

The Brython Compiler

Python has multiple code compilers, but Brython is one of the best compilers which converts code written in Python into JavaScript language. This extraordinary compiler has unique capability to transform the code and work as editor to achieve results speedily.

Furthermore, it offers assistance for a couple of module,s having a spot with the CPython. It is very supportive of many other languages and their new versions.

It is used for customer-side web programming. Brython is a compression for Browser Python. It flaunts an extensive usefulness, from making straightforward record components and moving to 3D route. The Python compiler prefers to be run in Firefox over Google Chrome. Brython offers help for every single present-day program, and is versatile for all internet browsers.

As indicated by the official blog of Pierre Quentel, Brython's maker and lead designer, Brython is a lot quicker than Pypy.js and Skulpt. In specific cases, the Python compiler is considerably speedier than the Python reference usage. For example, CPython.

Brython bolsters the more significant part of the sentence structure of Python 3, such as perceptions, generators, and imports. Additionally, it offers help for a few modules having a place with the CPython dissemination and accompanies libraries to cooperate with DOM components and occasions.

The Nuitka Compiler
Nuitka is another compiler of Python that takes code written in Python language as input and transforms it into C language to execute it. The Nuitka compiler is accessible for' many operating systems and platforms. It is an updated compiler that is very friendly to windows, mac and other operating systems.

It is conceivable to utilize Nuitka for creating independent projects, notwithstanding when you are not running Python on your machine.

Composed totally in Python, Nuitka permits utilizing different Python libraries and expansion modules. Nuitka is additionally accessible with Anaconda for those leaning toward it for creating tasks including information science and AI.

The PyJS Compiler

PyJS Compiler is a different kind of Python compiler. The professionals in the programming field mostly use it. It changes the code written in Python into javascript. It is especially used to run code in web programs.

PyJS provides runtime support, which is why it is recommended for web-based programs. For those hoping to compose Python code and execute it in internet browsers, PyJS is one of the go-to alternatives. The PyJS compiler interprets Python code into a proportionate JavaScript code with the goal that it can execute inside an internet browser.

A significant part of PyJS is that it accompanies an AJAX system that fills the holes left among JS and DOM bolster accessible for various internet browsers.

It is conceivable to run a Python web application source code as an independent work area application (that keeps running under Python) utilizing the PyJS Desktop module. Interestingly, Several Unix frameworks highlight preinstalled PyJS and PyJS Desktop variants.

Regardless of the contrasts among Python and JavaScript, a large portion of the information types are indistinguishable among the two prevalent programming dialects. While utilizing PyJS, a part of the

Python information types are changed over to custom articles, for example, records.

PyJS is a lightweight application. Additionally, it tends to be utilized legitimately from the internet browser and permits executing programs from an internet browser. The PyJS compiler offers runtime support for runtime blunders. As it is conceivable to insert Python code in the JS code. JS engineers can plan and create applications in an unadulterated article arranged worldview utilizing PyJS.

The Shed Skin Compiler

It transforms a statically created code of Python into a proportionate, unadulterated C++ program. Shed Skin doesn't offer assistance for some regular highlights, using settled limits and describing limits that recognize variable arguments. Very few libraries are used with this compiler.

Shed Skin is used to disentangle statically formed code in Python into revised code of C/C++ language with a couple of repressions. Using Shed Skin is beneficial because it is about essential display support. It is essentially a direct result of the way that the Python compiler has re-actualized the worked in data types into one of a kind plan of classes, executed in compelling C++ code.

The Skulpt Compiler

Skulpt has in-program use of Python and modules. This compiler runs the written code directly in the web-browser, making code more executable in runtime. This Skulpt compiler is introduced into a present blog or site page also. SKULPT code is also used in HTML. Written in JavaScript and accessible under the MIT permit, Skulpt offers a real situation where the gathered code is executed in the JS structure.

Since Skulpt is an in-program usage of Python, there is no requirement for extra preparing, modules, or server-side help required for running Python in an internet browser. Any Python code written in Skulpt is straightforwardly executed in the internet browser.

Skulpt is a decent choice for engineers hoping to make a web application that enables clients to run Python programs inside an internet browser while keeping the foundation servers secure. The well-known Python compiler can be effectively implanted into a current blog or website page as well.

For custom coordination, Skulpt code can be added to the HTML. You can likewise instruct Skulpt how to import your one of a kind custom modules for having more control. Although Skulpt makes an interpretation of Python code into JS code, it doesn't encourage running this.

The WinPython Compiler

WinPython is made for the Windows working framework. Its previous version has many bugs, and they were not well-planned compilers for the windows operating system. WinPython was brought forth as a response to the issue. Despite the way that the present emphasis of CPython is significantly enduring on the Windows working framework, it has a couple of select highlights. It is free transport for Python; you need download and empty it to start. It comes pre-packaged with likely the most well-known Machine Learning and Data science Python libraries.

8.3 Python IDEs

An IDEs (Integrated Development Environment) is for the development of programming, and incorporates a few instruments explicitly intended for programming development. These apparatuses typically include:

- An editorial manager designed to deal with code (with, for instance, linguistic structure featuring, and auto-culmination)

- Manufacture, execution, and troubleshooting apparatuses

- Some source control

Most IDEs bolster a wide range of programming dialects and contain a lot more highlights. They can, in this manner, be huge and set aside some effort to download and introduce. You may likewise need propelled information to utilize them appropriately.

Conversely, a committed code manager can be as primary as a content tool with linguistic structure featuring and code designing abilities. Most great code editors can execute code and control a debugger. The absolute best ones cooperate with source control frameworks also. Contrasted with an IDE, a great devoted code supervisor is usually smaller and faster.

Incorporated Development Environment shortened IDE is characterized as a coding apparatus that helps to mechanize the marvel of altering, assembling, testing, and so forth in an SDLC, and it gives a straightforwardness to the engineer to run, compose and investigate the code.

Some Python IDEs include:

- PyCharm
- Spyder
- PyDev
- Atom
- Wing
- Jupyter Notebook
- Thonny
- Microsoft Visual Studio
- Eric Python

The PyCharm IDEs

A cross-stage PyCharm IDE- Integrated Development Environment extraordinarily intended for Python. It is utilized worldwide and accessible in both paid form and free open-source.

PyCharm is a complete IDE with unique features, like auto code fruition, brisk venture route, quick mistake checking and remedy, remote advancement support, and database availability.

Salient Features:

- Provides efficient code route
- Highlights errors significantly
- Effective debugging.

The Spyder IDEs

It is best for data scientist, as it is an open-source IDE. The complete name of Spyder is Scientific Python Development Environment. It is supported by Linux, Windows, and macOS X. Spyder comes included with the Anaconda bundle director dispersion, so depending upon your arrangement, you may already have it on your machine.

What's fascinating about Spyder is that it's intended interest group is information researchers utilizing Python. For instance, Spyder coordinates well with standard Python information science libraries like SciPy, NumPy, and Matplotlib.

Spyder includes the vast majority of the "basic IDE functions" you may expect. For example, a code manager with strong language structure featuring Python code fulfillment, and even an incorporated documentation program.

A different element that I haven't seen in other Python altering conditions is Spyder's "variable voyager" that enables you to show information utilizing a table-based design directly inside your IDE. By and by, I more often than not don't require this; however, it looks flawless. On the off chance that you routinely do information science work utilizing Python, you may become hopelessly enamored with this remarkable element. The IPython/Jupyter combination is also decent.

By and large, I'd state that Spyder feels more essential than different IDEs. I like to see it more as a specific reason device as opposed to something I use as my critical altering condition each day. What is decent about this Python IDE is that it is accessible on Windows, macOS, and Linux and that it is an entirely open-source program.

- Proper quality Syntax

- IPython Integrated

The PyDev IDE

It is the most demanded Python IDE. For Python developers, it is an undeniable IDE. Pydev has a component which incorporates Django combination, programmed code fruition, shrewd indents, and square indents.

Accessible for Linux, Windows, and OS X, Eclipse is the accepted open-source IDE for Java advancement. It has a vibrant commercial center of expansions and additional items, which makes Eclipse helpful for a broad scope of advanced exercises.

One such expansion is PyDev, which empowers Python investigating, code finish, and intuitive Python support. Introducing PyDev into Eclipse is simple: from Eclipse, select Help, Eclipse Marketplace, at that point scan for PyDev. Click Install and restart Eclipse.

Cons: If you're beginning with Python, or with programming improvement, all in all, Eclipse can be a great deal.

Salient Features:

- Code inspection and verification.

- Contain PyLint combination, remote debugger, Unit test joining.

The Atom IDE

It is the most popular IDE made by GitHub. It is an open-source and cross-platform. First, the package of IDE is downloaded. When you have arranged the software on your machine, you can begin working on coding to initiate the project. The instructional exercise briefs you about all the functions, step-by-step. A coordinated advancement enables you to begin highly integrated work between the software. The instructional exercise, likewise, acquaints you with Python's mainframe software. Be that as it may, Jupyter Notebook isn't the best alternative for true ventures. A code supervisor would it be advisable for you to utilize.

Atom is highly recommended for multiple platform code management and effectively editing of code during the live programs.

Its designers consider it a less secure tool. Particle empowers clients to introduce outsider bundles and topics to alter the highlights. In any case, Atom is incredible for information science, enabling you to work with high-level programming languages.

Salient Features:

- It shows the results in runtime windows.

- It has a module "Markdown Preview Plus"

The Wing IDE

This version is free. The star rendition accompanies a 30-day preliminary trial for developers. It has a few functions that incorporate auto-fulfillment, sentence structure features, indents, etc.

It assesses information within stacked software data systems, or by drifting over images in the editorial manager. It investigates the document, thoroughly generating results.

Restrictive Breakpoints

Restrictive and overlook included breakpoints are utilized in the program and are frequently re-used in the same program to confine and settle errors influencing a specific software. It likewise stops consequently, while some uncertain circumstances appear.

Moreover, it is a vital debugger that works fast. With regards to the current troubleshoot stack outline, it has multi-purpose modules.

Salient Features:

- Customizable and can have expansions.

- It supports remote advancement, test-driven improvement alongside the unit test.

Jupyter Notebook IDE

Jupyter was created on the server-customer structure and enables you to make and control note pad reports. Jupyter Notebook was conceived out of IPython in 2014. It is a web application dependent on the server-customer structure, and it enables you to make and control note pad archives - or just "scratchpad".

You should give it a shot because Jupyter Notebook furnishes you with a simple to utilize, intuitive information science condition crosswise over many programming dialects that doesn't just fill in as an IDE. It's ideal for individuals who are merely beginning with information science!

Highlights The Jupyter Notebook allows you to add HTML segments from pictures to recordings. On account of Jupyter, you can without much of a stretch see and alter your code to make convincing introductions. For example, you can utilize information perception libraries, like Matplotlib and Seaborn, and demonstrate your charts in a similar archive where your code is. In addition, you can send out your last work to PDF and HTML records, or you can trade it as a .py document. Likewise, you can also make online journals and introductions from your scratchpad.

Jupyter Notebook ought to be a fundamental piece of any Python information researcher's tool compartment. It's extraordinary for prototyping and imparting scratchpad to representations.

Salient Features:

- Jupyter notebooks has a feature of supporting markdowns

- Codes can be generated and changed easily

- Best for beginners in the data science field

Thonny IDE

If you want to learn and instruct programming languages, then this IDE is another way of doing it. Thonny is mostly used by the beginners and considered as easy to understand IDE. It is a prevalent development environment in the Python data science community.

Salient Features:

- Debugging is easy and straightforward.

- It contains features of auto code finish along with featuring blunders.

Microsoft Visual Studio IDE

It is best suited for improving and investigating web activities. It is an open-source code generator accessible to all the programmers across the world.

Salient Features:

- It allows Python coding in visual studio, which is a unique feature of this IDE.

- It is available in paid form as well as free.

Why IDEs and Code Editors?

Why do you need an IDE or a code editorial manager? You can generally push directions on a command-line terminal and execute your projects, regardless of whether R or Python. Notwithstanding, doing this for enormous programming tasks can be quite disappointing - mainly if you aren't used to the direction line translator applications. Using an IDE or a decent code editorial manager can make coding simpler and fun. They are coding devices that enable you to compose, test, and troubleshoot your code. IDEs and code editors are the best approach for speedy work. They can deal with code charitably and include code auto-finishing, sentence structure featuring, and troubleshooting devices.

8.4 Python Text Editor

Sublime Text

Sublime text editor is full of functionalities. It is an editing program software written in C++ language, and also used for Python. Its updated version and supports multiple languages. Jon Skinner created it, and it was added to the market in 2007. To make this item, he followed three rules:

- Discreet, remote interface: we ought to have the alternative to prioritize content and avoid multiple tools.

- The content isn't concealed by the windows.

- Use all available space that could sensibly be normal: through full-screen usage, it makes for easy editing.

This Text editor, as part of Python IDE, has all essential functions of anytothe universal editor software. It gives easy access to formatting tools and making an automatic attempt to restructure the text for allowing the process to complete smoothly.

Salient Features
- Quick and small amount of bugs

- Opens gigantic records

- Supports many programming dialects

Vim Text Editor

Vim text editor is a popular editing tool for Python. It was developed in 1991 by Bram Moolenaar. This editor is used to restructure and redesign text files. Vim contrasts other content editors in its secluded strategy for action. It has multiple modes to manipulate the text. It is a free, high demand programming software, and is customizable by including extensions or changing its plan record. In other words, it infers one can use it without a lot of modification. Vim has three primary modes: implant mode, commonplace or request mode, and course line mode.

Salient Features:

- Software is rich in features and gives excellent client involvement with network connectivity.

- Transformation of document positions in operating systems can be done quickly through Vim text editor.

GNU/Emacs Text Editor

It is a highly recommended GNU/Emacs Text Editor that was developed by Richard Stallman. It remained prevalent among the programming professionals for almost 20 years. The owner of the program made it free for every user. Editing MACros- Emacs is an exclusive member of the text editors' family. This software helps Python programming in gaining high-tech features. GNU Emacs uses unique customization contents for progression in a couple of programming languages.

The Elpy extension of this editor has many attractive features, including sentence structure to separate record segments, and spaces between text to have solid orchestrating in an archive.

Salient Features:

- Free and movable programming

- Automatic expansion of segments needed for record structure.

- Multiple operating systems with 24-bit color support.

Chapter 9

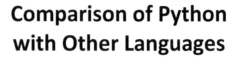

Comparison of Python with Other Languages

Python can be compared with other high-level programming languages. In comparison to other languages, Python surpasses based on functionalities, methods, libraries, and user-friendliness. This language has professional modules, frameworks and translators that are increasing its popularity among the software industry and IT professionals. These correlations focus on the credibility of programming code and other significant factors. Let's discuss the detailed comparison of Python with other programming languages.

9.1 Python versus Java comparison

Java programs are faster than Python programs. Python is vastly improved as a "high-level" language, while Java is better described as a low-level execution language. Indeed, the two together make a superb mixture. Various Segments can be generated in Java and joined to shape usage in Python. Python can be utilized to model parts until their structure can be "solidified" in a Java usage. A Python program written in Java is considered half-developed, which permits calling Python code from Java and the other way around. In this execution, Python source code is meant Java bytecode (with assistance from a runtime library to help Python's dynamic semantics).

Java is a carefully embodied language, which means the variable names must be unequivocally proclaimed. Interestingly, we have a progressively composed Python, where no affirmation is required. There are numerous questions about powerful and measurement producing in programming languages. Notwithstanding, one idea ought to be noted: Python is an adaptable language with straightforward sentence structure, which makes it a superb answer for composing contents and rapidly creating applications for different fields.

Java enables you to make cross-platform applications, while Python is good with practically all cutting edge working frameworks. Regarding start, Java is unreasonably convoluted for tenderfoots contrasted with Python. Furthermore, the simplicity of perusing code is better with Python. When you require your code to be executed from anyplace, at that point, pick Java. The other bit of leeway of Java is that it gives you a chance to make organized based applications, while Python can't.

Java is considerably more convoluted than Python. When you don't have any specialized foundation learning, Java won't be simple. Then again, Java is utilized to program for various conditions and runtime executions of the program.

9.2 Python versus C#

Regarding effortlessness, Python was initially made to look like English discourse. Such vast numbers of articulations in it are anything but difficult to peruse, mainly if you utilize appropriate variable names. Moreover, because of basic grammar, there are no entangled developments, for example, syntactic sections, countless word-modifiers, different C-like developments, and various approaches to introduce factors. Everything makes the code written in Python simple for comprehension and learning.

Simultaneously, C#, because of the language heredity, has loads of things from C++ and Java, which is at first communicated in C-like sentence structure. Also, C# language structure makes it essential to adhere to specific standards when composing your techniques or acquiring classes, which is joined by another surge of word-modifiers. One shouldn't likewise disregard squares of code, which ought to be 'enclosed' in props. Python doesn't have everything; it uses shifts which additionally make the code look perfect.

Concerning the code programming composition, it's likely worth referencing that projects which Python calls code are codes, they are merely recording with code that can be effectively executed by the mediator. One can open them in any manager, work with them, and after that, quickly run once more. Also, with Python it's a lot simpler to compose cross-platform contents which don't should be recompiled.

In Python programming language, we can design the required function to translate the code by machine and can shift this code to other platforms or systems to get executed. This cross-platform feature of this programming language is unique. Subsequently, it will build the size of the content from a few kilobytes to twelve megabytes. Not helpful for one-time use.

Thus, C # requires IDE for typical programming. As an or more of C#, it has a reliable help for different segments of the Windows framework when you are composing content for Windows. For instance, there are worked in devices for working with the library, WMI, the system, etc. Also, C# enables you to utilize WinForms, which makes it extremely simple to create a graphical interface if it is all of a sudden, required all things considered.

There is no right answer what language Python or C# is better. Python is simpler to learn; it has a lot increasingly open-source libraries contrasted with C#. However, the standard library of C# is superior to Python's, C# has more functions, its presentation is higher, and it advances truly quick.

9.3 Python versus Javascript

Python's "object-based" subset is commonly corresponding to JavaScript. Like JavaScript (and not at all like Java), Python reinforces a programming style that uses fundamental limits and factors without participating in class definitions. Regardless, for JavaScript, there is always a need for class participation. Python, on the other hand, supports making much higher ventures and better code reuse through a genuine article orchestrated programming style, where classes and heritage expect a critical activity.

9.4 Python versus Perl

Python and Perl start from a near establishment (Unix scripting, which both have long outgrown), and sport various equivalent features, anyway, have a substitute perspective. Perl stresses support for typical application- assignments, for example, by having worked in common explanations, investigating records, and report creating features. Python underlines support for essential programming strategies, for instance, data structure plan and thing organized programming and urges programming architects to create understandable (and along these lines reasonable) code by giving a rich anyway not unreasonably cloud documentation. Subsequently, Python approaches Perl yet on occasion beats it in its one of a kind application territory; in any case, Python has a genuine nature well past Perl's claim to fame.

9.5 Python versus Tcl

Tcl likewise to Python is used as an application development language, similarly as a free programming language. In any case, Tcl, which for the most part, stores all data as strings, is frail on data structures, and executes conventional code significantly more delayed than Python. Tcl in like manner needs features required for creating vast activities, for instance, estimated namespaces. Along these lines, while a "regular" immense application using Tcl, as a rule, contains Tcl enlargements written in C or C++ that are express to that application, a related Python application can much of the time be written in "Complete Python Code." Tcl's one of the redeeming qualities is the Tk tool compartments, whereas Python has gotten an interface to Tk as its standard GUI portion library.

9.6 Python versus Smalltalk

Possibly the best differentiation among Python and Smalltalk is Python's progressively "standard" language structure, which allows software experts an ease in working. Like Smalltalk, Python has dynamic forming, which is increasing the usage and functionalities of this programming language. Nevertheless, Python perceives worked in object types data from customer described classes. However; Smalltalk's standard library data types is dynamically refined.

Python's library has more workplaces for overseeing Internet and WWW substances, for instance, email, HTML, and FTP.

176

Python can store both standard modules and customer modules in individual records, which can be improved or coursed outside the framework. There is more than one decision for affixing a Graphical User Interface (GUI) to a Python program, whereas Smalltalk lacks this attribute.

9.7 Python versus C++

Python and C++ are the programming languages used for the development of high-level projects. Both Python and C++ languages vary from one another from numerous points of view. C++ is begun from C language with various ideal models and gives multiple in-built components for creating programs, whereas Pyhton is similar to English language with highly simple syntax.

Python is a universally useful and one of the high-level programming languages. A variable can be utilized straightforwardly without its presentation while composing code in Python.

In C++, a separate program needs to get ordered on each working framework on which the code is to be executed, while Python has frameworks that allow users to run a program in small sections

Python gives the capacity to 'compose, and run on any platform' that empowers it to keep running on all the working frameworks.

C++ is inclined to memory spill as it doesn't give separate execution option and uses pointers to a vast degree.

Python has inbuilt trash accumulation and dynamic memory portion process that empowers proficient use of memory.

C++, nowadays, is commonly utilized for planning equipment. It is first portrayed in C++ pursued by its examination, structurally compelled, and wanted to build up a register-move level equipment depiction language.

Python is utilized as a scripting language, and now It is also used for the non-scripting reason. Likewise, Python has an independent executable application with the assistance of some built-in functions.

9.8 Python versus Common Lisp and Scheme

Common Lisp and Scheme are close to Python in their dynamic semantics. Python has logical limits like those of Lisp. Their programs can have unlimited consistent conditions to perform a particular task of extended length. Common Lisp and Scheme have some complex variations in their coding schemes only understandable by programmers. In contrast, Python has simple, easy to understand, and straightforward coding to manage every line of code.

9.9 Python vs. Golang

Golang is quite an adaptable language, just like Python. Both the languages do not require excessive instructional exercise and are easy to understand and executable. Golang is also called Go language, and Google developed it in 2009.

Python underpins numerous programming ideal models and has a vast standard library; ideal models included are object-oriented, basic, practical, and procedural.

Go underpins multi-worldview like procedural, practical, and simultaneous. Its sentence structure is customarily originating from C; however, it has a smooth syntax structure, which requires less effort.

It is observed that Python and 'Go' have too many differences. Take for example Golang doesn't use the feature of *try-except,* rather it allows functions to show problems together with a conclusion. Therefore, before using a function, it is required to check that error will not return. Python is mostly utilized in web applications, whereas Golang prime focus is to become a system language. However, go is also utilized in some web applications. Python has no memory management, but Golang provides efficient memory management. Python does not have a concurrency mechanism, whereas Golang, on the other hand, has a built-in concurrency mechanism.

In terms of safety, Python is a strongly typed language which is compiled, so it adds an extra layer of security whereas Go is not too bad since each factor must have a sort related with it. It implies a designer can't let away the subtleties, which will further prompt bugs.

Python has a greater number of libraries than Golang. Python is more concise than Golang. Python is the best option for basic programming, as it gets difficult to write complicated functions with it. However, Golang is much better in complex programming than Python

Not only this, there is also one significant dissimilarity exists. Python is a language that can be typed dynamically, whereas Go is not dynamic.

The main reason behind the fact is that Python developers can easily understand Golang without any problem.

1. Python focuses on simple and clear syntax, and spotless grammar of Go drives correctly to high clarity.

2. The static composting of Go lines up with the standard of "express is superior to understood" in Python.

So it can be said that Python is the best option for software engineers and developers all around the globe. But because Python is dynamically typed language, its performance is lesser than Golang due to its uniqueness of statically typed. Therefore it is better to use both languages simultaneously. For coding, give priority to Golang and use Python otherwise.

Python versus Node.js
It's critical to recollect that Node.js isn't a programming language like Python, yet instead a runtime domain for JavaScript.

Hence, writing in Node.js means you're utilizing a similar language on the frontend and the backend.

Favorable circumstances of Python over Node.js
At a further advanced level, JavaScript can be hard to comprehend for developers with less Node.js experience. They may commit some genuinely basic errors, hindering progress simultaneously.

It isn't the situation with Python, since it's simpler to use for less experienced developers. The slip-ups made by them will have, to a lesser extent, a negative effect on improvement.

Lower section point
Frameworks, for example, Django is supportive, increment the nature of your code, and accelerate the way toward composing.

More applications

Node.js is, for the most part, utilized for the web, while the uses of Python are far more noteworthy.

The all-inclusiveness and flexibility of Python are among the top reasons why the language is an excellent fit for slanting advancements, for example, data science.

Better usage

JavaScript runtime conditions and frameworks all unexpectedly actualize the language; Node.js is no exemption. In all honesty, the ecosystem of JavaScript is somewhat of a wreck—however, not even close as terrible as it used to be.

Python doesn't have that issue, which is the reason it's more straightforward and simpler to utilize. It additionally makes the language quicker to write in, although Node.js is not slow.

It's crucial to know JavaScript if you wish to utilize Node.js since you're managing a similar language on the frontend and the backend.

Less obstinate ecosystem

Node.js has unique features that it pushes developers through indicators about "what they need to use and when they need to use" when they are working through this programming language.

It has a lot of built-in packages that developers need to understand. That's why, with the improvement of programming libraries, the developers will have to develop their skills to that level.

Coding everything in JavaScript

The javascript is used for frontend and backend programming with the assistance of Node.js to achieve the best results. It saves a lot of time and makes the work easy for users. Nowadays, IT experts use this language as much as possible to perform web-based programming tasks.

Quick development and huge network

Since 2012, Python has been reliably lauded for its incredible network and support—and which is all well and good. With its large number of libraries and frameworks, it has quick development procedures by calling the required library or function.

Nowadays, JavaScript is similarly also upheld. It continues developing without any indications of halting and stays particularly ahead of the pack of the most powerfully growing languages in the business.

Advancement history of Python and JavaScript

JavaScript has seen a lot of developing agonies. Its code was rejected many times when it was created, and its old adaptations are as yet making similar issues today.

Overall, Python has the high ground here. The documentation and inclusion of Python are both better than Node.js. With regards to unwavering quality, Python has consistently been in front of JavaScript.

Inclining advances

The tumultuous ecosystem of JavaScript additionally makes Node.js excessively precarious and erratic to depend on for drifting innovations.

As a result of the critical issues of JavaScript patterns, JavaScript innovations become obsolete significantly more rapidly. It is the reason Node.js is an unsafe decision for rising innovative trends.

Python doesn't represent that hazard, since it presents significant changes gradually. The language is an ideal fit for slanting innovations, for example, machine learning or data science, with its first-class specialists and library support.

Execution and speed

Node.js may battle with executing a great deal of assignments immediately. The code isn't composed well overall; your program will perform ineffectively and work gradually.

It may occur with Python, but Python frameworks, for example, Django, provides instant support to assist your program to run smoothly.

It's one more case of Python making life easier for developers.

Your program quality is everything—it's the main factor to think about when choosing the programming language for your final product shape.

Python works better for certain undertakings and Node.js works better for other people. Your decision ought to depend completely on whether you have great Python or JavaScript developers in your group.

This contention is invalid on the off chance that you happen to have full-stack developers with the two programming languages;

nonetheless, those are difficult to find, so you need to decide your programming strategy before you start.

9.10 Python versus PHP

From the improvement perspective, PHP is a web-situated language. A PHP application is increasingly similar to a lot of exclusive content, possibly with a separate semantic section point.

Python is an adaptable language that can be additionally applied for web improvement. A web application dependent on Python is an undeniable application stacked into memory with its inside state, spared from the inquiry to the solicitation. Picking between Python or PHP for web applications focus on the following qualities:

Python versus PHP for web improvement correlation

Patterns and prevalence of a programming language are critical these days. A few clients and program proprietors need to utilize the most famous and advertised advancements for their undertakings. As PHP has command over web-application programming and widely used among the developer's community, it is considered the best option to achieve high-speed applications. Whereas Pythos also works for web-applications, the main agenda of this programming language is Data Science.

Frameworks

Python has a lot of functional libraries that are famous across the world, for example, Pandas, Numpy, and more. Similarly, there are highly efficient open-source code mechanisms. PHP has a different approach towards code quality and system of innovative addition in this programming source.

There are popular frameworks in Python, but the most useful are Django and Flask. Globally, developers are using these frameworks to enhance the speed of their work. PHP language doesn't use frameworks. Instead, it focuses on calling libraries built by other PHP communities.

It is an established reality that Python's framework will change soon because of the developing network of Python.

Chapter 10

Future of Python

Python is ruling the world of modern technology and due to its uniqueness it has left other languages like C++, Java, etc. far behind. Python, with its great utility, has a promising and bright future. Python has gone though 25 years of continuous amendments with improved and better-updated versions so that it can serve as the fastest and most reliable programming language. Python provides the best quality, which is why it catches the eye of every developer. Over 126,000 websites have utilized Python. A plethora of decision-making systems for predictive analysis have developed applications using Python. It is the language of today and the future, as well.

10.1 Profiles of Python developers

Python developers are as assorted as the language and its applications. Python clients vary broadly in age, yet most of its users are in their 20s, and a quarter are in their 30s. Strikingly, nearly one-fifth of Python clients are under the age of 20. It can be clarified, by the way, that numerous under-studies use Python in schools and colleges, and it's a common first language for many computer programmers.

According to the recent survey, almost 65% of software engineers are moving towards Python language as a career. As Python is a simple

186

and easy to learn language, many newcomers are adopting this high-level language to make their fortune from this new field of Data Science. It is a widespread practice nowadays and every software engineer is looking to learn the libraries, methods, and use of Python to become a data scientist. 30% of engineers that have under two years of expert experience have started using Python as their primary programming language.

General Python utilization

Right around four out of five Python designers state it's their primary language. Different research demonstrates the quantity of Python engineers, which are using it as primary language. In Stack Overflow's review, Python fame has expanded from 32% in mid-2017 to 38.8% by the end of that year.

Python utility with Other Languages:

Python is being used by all developers now who were only focusing on other high-level languages just a year ago. This trend is changing because of the evolution of Data Science.

According to a survey, JavaScript is utilized by 79% of web engineers, yet just 39% of those are engaged with Data investigation or Artificial Intelligence.

Some important companies that use Python as Data Science:

Google

Google is considered the biggest IT giant and has supported Python from its start. Google utilizes Python in their web crawler.

Facebook

Facebook is keen in utilizing Python in their Production Engineering Department.

Instagram

Instagram's engineering team revealed in 2016 that the world's most massive deployment of the Django web framework driven by them is completely written in Python.

Netflix

Netflix utilizes Python in a very similar manner to Spotify, depending on the language to power its data analysis on the server-side.

Dropbox

This cloud-based storage system employs Python in its desktop client.

10.2 Factors behind the Python growth in Modern World

Growth of Python is becoming prominent and is improving day by day. Software engineers and developers prefer this language due to its versatility and ease of use. Various other factors that are behind its growth are as follows:

1. Good support and community

Programming languages often face support issues. They lack complete documentation to help programmers when problems arise. Python has no such issues and is well supported. A plethora of tutorials and documentation is available to assist the programmers in the best possible ways. It has a good and active community whose function is to support developers. Experienced programmers help the beginners and a supportive atmosphere has been created.

2. Easy to Code and Write

If we compare Python to other programming languages like Java, C or C++, Python possesses a readable and straightforward code. Coding is expressed in a relatively easy manner to allow beginners to understand it quickly.

To learn the advanced level of python programming, a lot of time and effort is required, but for beginners, it is an easy task. Users can quickly identify the purpose of code, even after a quick glance.

3. Python is the Language of Education

Python is an easy language to use. It possesses functions, expressions, variables, and all other elements that students can easily understand and practice. It is the standard programming language for the Raspberry Pi, a PC structured training. Colleges teach Python in PC sciences, as well as to arithmetic understudies. Also, Matplotlib (a prominent Python library) is utilized in subjects at all levels to express complex data. Python is one of the quickest developing languages on Codecademy, as well, and thus is anything but difficult to learn remotely.

4. Simple to Code and Write

Python has an elementary coding and syntax structure. In comparison to other high-level programming languages like Java, C, or C++, Python has a straightforward and discernible code. The code is communicated in a simple way, which can be mostly deciphered even by a novice software engineer.

5. Python Is Perfect For Building Prototypes.

Python not only allows the users to write less code, it also provides the utility to build prototypes and ideas very quickly. Brainstorming or ideation is an essential aspect of web development, which is mostly overlooked. The capability to think about prototypes that can function faster becomes much more pivotal.

6. Integration and execution is quick

Python is considered as high-class language. It is the quickest language when it comes to execution and integration and saves quite a lot of time for programmers. With projects like PyPy and Numba, the speed is enhanced even more, making it the fastest language with each passing day.

7. Python has a Standard Library

Python contains libraries that eliminate the burden of composing a code by the programmer. These libraries possess a large quantity of built-in functions and already available codes. Therefore, code can easily be generated instead of having to be created.

8. Cross-Platform Language

One of the most prominent features of Python Programming Language is that it is accessible to cross-platforms. It supports highly efficient operating systems such as Linux, Windows, Ubuntu, and more.

Thus, one can undoubtedly keep running a product without agonizing over framework support. It very well may be translated in the language with the assistance of a convenient component that makes it easy to utilize. To sum things up - compose code on the Mac and run it smoothly on Windows.

9. Provides a plethora of tools

It contains a vast standard library collection, which reduce the effort for writing codes or functions. Libraries in Python always have pre-written codes in them.

Some of the tools are as follows: Tkinter (a GUI development), file format, built-in function, custom Python interpreter, internet protocols and support, module, etc. This extensive collection increases the usefulness of Python as a programming tool for data science.

10. Python is Free

Python is an open-source language and its free to use. Guido van Rossum has run Python since its creation. It is Open Source and GPL excellent. The creator of this language had a vision to keep it free for all the programmers of the world. However, open-source programming has officially changed the world. Python has no hidden cost or sale-able modules, and this makes it an ideal device for all to utilize.

10.3 Career Opportunities Associated With Python

In this powerful present-day world where everything changes at a quick rate, the prevalence of Python never seems to stop. Today, Python Certification is very popular. It has a lot of libraries that help data investigation, control, and representation. In this manner, it has advanced as the most favored language and viewed as the "Following Big Thing" and an "Absolute necessity" for Professionals.

With a wide range of programming languages, Python has outperformed different languages. Vocation openings related to Python have additionally developed fundamentally as its fame has expanded. Numerous IT organizations are searching for more applicants with experience and aptitudes in Python programming languages. Python has shown to be the best vocation for software engineers and now is the time - sooner rather than later.

Conclusion

Python is a famous object-oriented language that is highly compatible with data science. In today's world, many companies are making their data management systems more advance with the ability to predict future outcomes through the use of the Python programming language. Python contains the best features, including a broad set of functions, libraries, expressions, arrays modules, statements, etc. Python usage is not limited to a particular field, such as web programming. Therefore, it is known as a *multipurpose* programming language. Hundreds of data scientists, top companies, software engineers, and accountancy firms are giving preference to Python over all other programming languages. This high-level programming language is being used in every kind of application, including web application and game application. The data management field is growing rapidly, making it possible to design predictive models for mega enterprises. Understanding Python is one of the significant abilities required for a data science profession. This high-level programming language has evolved as a data analysis tool over. Here's a brief history:

- In 2016, it surpassed R on Kaggle, the chief stage for data science rivalries.

- In 2017, it surpassed R on KDNuggets' yearly survey of data scientists' most utilized devices.

- In 2018, 66% of data scientists revealed using Python day by day, making it the central apparatus for data scientists.

The experts predicted a 35% increase in demand for data scientists by the year 2021. It is the right time to develop your skill in this highly demanded programming language for data science, as it will raise your career to a new level. Every business is requiring efficient data analysis systems that get data, arrange it, and convert it into useful information. The data scientist who can build up a professional predictive system by using Python programming can make a difference in every business. In this big data era, data professionals will become the most essential individuals for all businesses across the world.

References

1- Basics of Python Data Science, 2019, "Programming language's uses" retrieved from https://www.javatpoint.com/

2- Best practices of programming and data analysis, 2017, "Python as data analysis tool" retrieved from https://hackr.io/blog

3- Syntax and role of coding, 2018, "Easy to learn coding", retrieved from https://hackernoon.com/

4- Importance of Machine learning, 2019, "Future of Data Science" retrieved from https://www.newgenapps.com/#1

5- Python Libraries and methods, 2018, "Data mechanisms under Python commands", retrieved from https://www.probytes.net/blog/Python-future/

6- How to write a Python functions, 2019, "Python functions and their use" retrieved from https://www.datacamp.com/

7- Mastering over Python Main data library,2019, "Pandas as main library", retrieved from https://towardsdatascience.com/

8- Comparison of Python with other high-level languages, 2018, "Python as advance data science language, retrieved from https://worthwhile.com/insights/2016/07/19/django-Python-advantages/

www.ingramcontent.com/pod-product-compliance
Lightning Source LLC
LaVergne TN
LVHW051231050326
832903LV00028B/2341